NEGOTIATING CRITICAL LITERACIES WITH TEACHERS

Theoretical Foundations and Pedagogical Resources for Pre-service and In-service Contexts

Vivian Maria Vasquez
Stacie L. Tate
Jerome C. Harste

 Routledge
Taylor & Francis Group

NEW YORK AND LONDON

First published 2013
by Routledge
711 Third Avenue, New York, NY 10017

Simultaneously published in the UK
by Routledge
2 Park Square, Milton Park, Abingdon, Oxon OX14 4RN

Routledge is an imprint of the Taylor & Francis Group, an informa business

Library of Congress Cataloging in Publication Data
Vasquez, Vivian Maria.
Negotiating critical literacies with teachers: theoretical foundations and
pedagogical resources for pre-service and in-service contexts / Vivian Maria
Vasquez, Stacie L. Tate, Jerome C. Harste.
pages cm
Includes bibliographical references and index.
1. Teachers—Training of—United States. 2. Teachers—In-service
training—United States. 3. Language arts—Social aspects—United States.
4. Literacy—Social aspects—United States. 5. Critical pedagogy—
United States. I. Title.
LB1715.V37 2013
370.71'1—dc23   2012033683

ISBN: 978-0-415-64161-6 (hbk)
ISBN: 978-0-415-64162-3 (pbk)
ISBN: 978-0-203-08177-8 (ebk)

Typeset in Bembo
by Book Now Ltd, London

SUSTAINABLE
FORESTRY
INITIATIVE
Certified Sourcing
www.sfiprogram.org
SFI-01234
SFI label applies to the text stock

Printed and bound in the United States of
America by IBT Global

DEDICATION

VV   To Dorothy—Teacher Extraordinaire.

SLT To Mom and Dad and all my students past and present.

JH   To the kind of teaching that simply takes your breath away.

CONTENTS

LIST OF FIGURES

PREFACE

This book is a response to a gap in the literature on critical literacy and teacher education. Specifically, this book speaks to what Dozier et al. (2006) observe as a profession that has not publicly articulated the nature of the alignment between our expectations for our own literate lives and our expectations for our students as literacy learners.

We view critical literacy and this book as a demonstration of our practices in attempting to create spaces for our students and the teachers with whom we work to consider ways of taking up critical literacies in their own lives both in and outside of school. This includes the theoretical orientations that we use in not only teaching our students about critical literacy but how to be practitioners who live critically literate lives. Our goal is for teachers, students, and those who take part in professional development events to participate differently in the world and to make the best informed decisions they could possibly make. Readers have to realize the power of their actions. Reading, reflecting, and discussing what is critical literacy is not enough. We believe that a full articulation of this practice comes with praxis. As professors of education, we teach our students about critical literacy but we also practice the tenets of this practice. This practice has often called us to give a voice to the voiceless, to speak and talk about injustice when no one in the room is willing to speak on this issue and to create counter narratives in order to disrupt dominant ideas about literacy and literacy learning. This book represents how each of us has wrestled to make critical literacy not just a part of our teaching practice but our lives.

We will show how the theorized practice of critical literacies in our university classrooms and professional development settings has not only informed our teaching but also changed our lives and the lives of our students. The questions that we ponder in this book, such as what does it mean to negotiate critical literacies and what does it mean to frame ones practice from a critical literacy perspective, illuminates the praxis of what we advocate for in this book. We want to demonstrate how we have created spaces and opportunities to experience first hand what it is like to be a learner, teacher, or researcher that has built their classroom philosophy or curriculum around their passions and interests.

Some of this material comes directly from the research we have done in classrooms, with teachers, and at professional developments for teachers throughout the United States and other countries. This book represents a coherent theorized practical narrative of what each of us has experienced inside and outside of the classroom with critical literacy. Throughout this book we present teacher narratives, pedagogical strategies, and points of reflections in order to enhance your experience with this text and to give you concrete examples and ideas of the importance of critical literacy in teacher education.

Chapters 1 and 2 outline various theoretical positions and learning theories that can inform a critical literacy curriculum, including inquiry learning, feminist perspectives, and other socio-cultural theories. We highlight the ways in which we work with students and teachers to build a theoretical toolkit as a way of helping them to better articulate why they do what they do in the classroom and why critical literacy matters. We also examine how we can negotiate spaces for critical literacy that fit into a literacy curriculum for the 21st century. Chapters 3 through 6 provide theorized practices of critical literacy such as building a curriculum around the interest of students, how the examination of children's literature can assist teachers and students in disrupting common ideologies often found in children's literature by creating counter-narratives that address dominate ideologies often found in this literature. We also look at how teachers develop their own framework and philosophy around critical literacy and finally we look at what media affords our teaching practices and how we can use technology and media to further negotiate a critical literacy perspective.

The final chapter of our book provides a deeply personal observation of our own history with critical literacy. We examine our lives, our own discursive practices, and how we have implemented the various ideas that we advocate for in our book. We conclude by arguing that, together, teachers and students need to explore and negotiate how to create spaces for critical literacies in their own settings.

ACKNOWLEDGMENTS

Thank you to my family especially my boys who made it easy to take a break from writing when it consumed me, and for supporting me unconditionally. To Dorothy Menosky, Barbara Comber, Hilary Janks, Sonia Nieto, Gerald Campano, Maria Paula Ghiso, and Carmen Medina—this book is about a way of being. I acknowledge you here because in your own way you have each taught me how to live in the academy with honor and ethics and I will always be grateful for that. To my amazing co-authors, Stacie and Jerry thank you for writing with me and for keeping the process of writing this book uncomplicated and an absolute pleasure! To Naomi Silverman the sun was shining when I met you and you have helped keep that sun shining through the years! Thank you for sustaining such enthusiasm for my work and for all that you have done to encourage and support me. I look forward to many more projects together!

Vivian Maria Vasquez

I am humbled to be able to write this book with two great academics—Dr. Vivian Vasquez and Dr. Jerry Harste. Never in my wildest dreams did I think that I would be writing with two of the most renowned names associated with critical literacy. I would like to thank both of you for being a great example of what it means to "live a critically literate life" in academia.

Stacie L. Tate

1

INTRODUCTION

In the summer of 2002, the people of Washington DC and the United States were invited by First Lady Laura Bush to "Take a Party Animal Safari" in the nation's capital. The Party Animals (see Figure 1.1), a public art project spearheaded by the DC Commission on the Arts and Humanities, consisted of 100 donkeys and 100 elephants, referred to as "rounded, full canvasses upon which artists expressed themselves" (Gittens, Woo, McSweeney, & Stovall, 2002, p. 17). According to the Commission, the Party Animals were about having a passion for art, not politics. For the most part people in the community and tourists consumed these art pieces in this way referring to the animals as fun, imaginative and whimsical. To encourage participation in the Party Animals art project, invitations were sent to thousands of artists to submit designs. While selecting the 200 chosen ones, the DC Commission noted that they were not looking for political statements but rather they were looking for fine public art. The sculptures were then scattered throughout DC where tourists and DC residents could go on safari to find as many party animals as possible.

In the fall of 2002, an announcement was made that the university where Vivian was working would be hosting a number of the party animals on campus. At the time Vivian was teaching reading and language arts courses to potential elementary school teachers. With her colleague, Sarah Jewett, she capitalized on her students' interest in the animals as an opportunity to have them re-read the sculptures from a critical literacy perspective.

What is powerful about this work, which is recounted in detail in Chapter 4, is the use of the students' interests to create spaces for critical literacies in a university classroom. In teacher education classes and in professional development workshops for classroom teachers, focused on critical literacy and inquiry

FIGURE 1.1 The Party Animals.

learning, participants are often reminded of the need to build curriculum using children's inquiry questions, passions and interests. More than often they hear this message or they are asked to read articles and books about what this means. What we are suggesting in this book is that there is more we could do to help pre-service and in-service teachers understand critical literacy. Rather than limiting what we do to telling (lectures) or showing (providing examples from other people's classrooms), we are suggesting giving them opportunities to experience firsthand what it is like to be a learner where the university teacher or workshop facilitator builds curriculum around their inquiry questions, passions and interests from a critical literacy perspective.

Living a Critically Literate Life

Negotiating Critical Literacies with Teachers is a demonstration of what it means to live a critically literate life. In particular this book puts on offer theoretical foundations and pedagogical resources for negotiating critical literacies in university or professional development settings as one way to help adult learners to not only learn about and frame their teaching from a critical literacy perspective but to help them live through or embody critical literacies that have importance in their own lives.

We wrote this book as a response to a gap in the literature on critical literacy and teacher education as well as teacher professional development. Specifically, this book speaks to what Dozier, Johnston and Rogers (2006) observe that as a profession we have not publicly articulated the nature of the alignment between our expectations for our own literate lives and our expectations for our students as literacy learners. This was reflected in the 1996 report of the National Commission on Teaching and America's Future, which noted that "… universities often do not practice what they preach in terms of teaching …" (p. 3). More recently Cahnmann-Taylor and Souto-Manning (2010) point out that we, as a teaching profession, need to avoid simply, "talking the talk" (p. 7). Vivian and Sarah, in their work with the Party Animals attempted to avoid simply talking the talk but having their students live rather than read or hear about a critical literacy curriculum.

We offer this book as a demonstration of our practices in attempting to create spaces for our students and the teachers with whom we work to consider ways of taking up critical literacies in their own lives and in and outside of school. This includes the theoretical orientations that we use in not only teaching our students about critical literacy but how to be practitioners that live critically literate lives. Our goal is for our students, and those who take part in our professional development events to be able to participate differently in the world and to make the most informed decisions they could possibly make about important social issues. In turn we hope these teachers are able to take what they experience with us back to their own settings for use with the children with whom they work.

Our Stories/Our Selves

The three of us have come together based on a common longstanding interest in creating spaces for critical literacies in our own settings. Stacie is currently an Assistant Professor at American University. She is a former middle and secondary classroom teacher. Vivian is currently a Professor at American University. She is a former early childhood and elementary school teacher. Jerry is now Professor Emeritus at Indiana University, Bloomington. He has been working alongside teachers and advocating for teachers for over forty years. Our cumulative experience, spans from working in pre-school to graduate school settings; from teaching toddlers to doctoral students. Our teaching practice focuses on teaching literacy courses and leading professional development workshops, institutes, and seminars. The focus of this book is the theorized practice of critical literacies in our university classrooms and professional development settings with adult learners.

How this Book is Organized

Since the main premise of the book is on ways to help pre-service and in-service teachers understand what it means to take on a critical literacy perspective as a way of being rather than as a set of activities, we thought it would be important for us to build into this text opportunities for you to engage with critical literacies yourselves. As such throughout the book we have included various points for reflection and discussion. These come in the form of reflection points, try this pedagogical strategies, and resource boxes.

REFLECTION POINT

Each reflection point focuses on a topic or issue. Some of these are set up as scenarios or contexts for you to discuss and think about. Others are set up as a series of questions for you to consider.

TRY THIS: Pedagogical Strategy

These take the form of invitations or activities to try in your setting, or narratives describing a particular engagement or strategy for taking up critical literacies in various contexts.

RESOURCE BOX

These are collections of texts that focus on a particular topic or issue. Some of these boxes are meant for use in professional development settings while others are materials such as text sets for use in classroom settings.

In order to make clear the theoretical positions from which we have written this book, in Chapter 2, "Negotiating Spaces for Critical Literacy in the 21st Century," we outline various theoretical positions and learning theories that can inform a critical literacy curriculum, including inquiry learning and other socio-cultural theories. We also include a beginning set of principles that might guide curriculum as we go about developing a more critically literate citizenry for the 21st century. In addition, as a way to make visible the life experiences that impact who we are, what we believe and our teaching practice, we have include author biographies at the end of Chapter 8, "Teaching and Living Critical Literacies." There we offer you a narrative account of some of our past experiences to give you a sense of the position(s) from which we speak and engage in the practice of teaching.

According to bell hooks (1994) teaching should be a career that engages not only the student but also the teacher. In Chapter 3, "Outgrowing Our Current Selves: It's Not Just a Job—It's a Lifestyle," we explore what it means to outgrow our current selves. In particular we focus on how the development and use of a teaching philosophy can help educators unpack their Discursive practices and the ideological positions through which they engage in the practice of teaching. These of course are the same positions through which they interpret their students' learning. Following this, in Chapter 4, "Building Curriculum Using Students' Interests," we pick up from where this introductory chapter began and further unpack what happened as space was created in Vivian's literacy methods class for her students to read the Party Animal sculptures from a critical literacy perspective. Their critical readings helped make visible the complexities, patterns, trends, particularities, generalities, and/or discrepancies, in the information conveyed on the sculptures. In Chapter 5, "Challenging Commonplace Thinking," we share instances of working with children's literature and everyday text such as print ads to disrupt the commonplace viewpoints. In this chapter we share examples of capitalizing on our students' interest in children's literature or adolescent novels as a jumping off point for constructing critical literacies in the tertiary classroom or workshop setting. This includes having participants re-design existing texts and creating counter-narrative texts or alternate version texts that disrupt the ideologies and dominant ideas that surround us. In the following chapter, "Interrogating Multiple Perspectives," we continue working with children's literature to explore possibilities for imagining the world from the perspective of others. This time however we focus heavily on the use of text sets or multiview texts. These are combinations of texts that offer complimentary or conflicting accounts of the same topic issue or event. In the chapter we talk about the ways in which multiple perspectives complicate what we know and thus complicate curriculum making for a much more sophisticated, powerful and pleasurable experience for our students.

Chapter 7 focuses on technology and media literacy. In this chapter we will talk about the possible relationship(s) between critical literacy and media studies by asking questions such as the following:

- What does new media afford our practice?
- Using technology, what can we do differently?
- Using technology, what can we do in new ways?

Also included in this chapter are examples of classroom explorations of critical literacy and media technology we share with our students and the teachers with whom we work.

In Chapter 8 we gather together final thoughts and set up a discussion on ways forward with regards to engaging with critical literacies as lived experiences with adult learners in pre-service or in-service settings. We share insights that tie together each of the chapters and in so doing lay down a course for future agendas. We argue for why education has to be more than rhetoric and that in order to be effective, learners need to take on new identities and new agency. We then discuss the notion that it is supporting the transformation of our selves and our world that needs to be the focus of curricular work in the future.

Education and Changing Culture

Education, like literacy, is never innocent. Even further, it is always about change, and even more specifically, cultural change. While one can argue that education should preserve culture, in reality education has always been about changing culture. The trick, we suppose, is to continually re-visit and re-think what we are doing. So, too, with literacy. We will conclude this introduction by arguing that together teachers and students need to explore how critical practices such as making social statements and taking social action can become a social practice embedded in classrooms of the 21st century because the future, after all, is ours for the making.

2

NEGOTIATING SPACES FOR CRITICAL LITERACY IN THE 21ST CENTURY

Carole Edelsky (1999) suggests that most of us have little or no conscious awareness of the socio-political systems of meaning that are operating and the power
relationships that are involved in what it is we teach. She believes that educators at
all levels need to negotiate spaces for critical literacy in their classrooms.

REFLECTION POINT 2.1

Current Understanding of Critical Literacy

- What is your current understanding of critical literacies?
- Say something about what you think of Edelsky's belief that educators at
  all levels should negotiate spaces for critical literacy in their classrooms.

Finding a Frame: Critical Literacy and Teacher Education—Why Does it Matter?

Although they don't use the term "critical literacy," Westheimer and Kahne (2004)
describe a range of political commitments associated with educating for democracy.
We have found their focus on citizenship as a frame for understanding curriculum
very helpful in illuminating various notions of critical literacy. They begin with
the definition of a "Personally Responsible Citizen." Such citizens, they tell us:
(1) Act responsibly in their community; (2) Work and pay taxes; (3) Obey laws;
(4) Recycle and give blood; and (5) Volunteer to lend a hand in times of crisis.

Given the problem of hunger in the community, for example, personally responsible citizens are willing to contribute their share to a food drive.

The next group they describe are "Participatory Citizens." From a critical perspective, participatory citizens do more than participate since they: (1) Take charge and organize community efforts; (2) Know how governments work; and (3) Implement strategies for accomplishing collective tasks. Given hunger as a problem in the community, participatory citizens would be the ones who would organize and lead the food drive.

Another citizenry that Westheimer and Kahne describe is labeled as "Justice-Oriented." Justice-oriented citizens: (1) Critically assess social, political, and economic structures to see beyond surface level causes; (2) Seek out and address areas of injustice; and (3) Know about democratic social movements and how to effect systemic change. In terms of responding to hunger as a community problem, justice-oriented citizens research why people don't have enough food and take social action to address root causes.

What is important about Westheimer and Kahne's model is that it stresses going beyond the surface structure of issues. When critical literacy is addressed in schools, we often stop at the level of a food drive or organizing a community campaign to collect money to fill a food pantry. While these are noble efforts, Westheimer and Kahne remind us that as educators, we should not be satisfied to produce personally responsible or even participatory citizens. Instead, we should aim for nothing less than sending forth justice-oriented citizens. The difference here is that justice-orientated citizens engage in sustained work to contribute to change that could have transformative effects for the communities in which they live and the people who live there.

Unpacking Critical Literacy

With a "justice-oriented citizenry" as our end goal and using the research on critical literacy as our base, we will make the case that critically literate individuals demonstrate some specific dispositions relative to their worldview. In short, they show an affinity for disrupting commonplace thinking, interrogating multiple perspectives, unpacking issues socio-politically, and taking social action for purposes of creating a more just and equitable world. At the same time, they understand (and are able to critique) their own complicity in maintaining the status quo.

Disrupting the Commonplace

Taking everyday practices and beliefs for granted is easy; disrupting what has been taken for granted is difficult. Disrupting the commonplace calls for a new level of conscious awareness. Things that seem normal need to be re-thought. Sociologist

Mary Douglas (in Eco, 1970) reminds us that common sense is cultural sense. In other words, whose culture gets to define "common sense" as *sensible*, makes a difference. In spite of all of the work done in the name of women's liberation, for example, women in our society typically still get less pay than males performing the same job. What this means is that despite the rhetoric of how much things have changed for women, there are still forces at work that ensure that women are kept down. Social scientists studying hiring practices have found that there is a "glass ceiling": Women now hold administrative positions in organizations, but they rarely hold the top administrative jobs. The term "glass ceiling" implies that there is a very real ceiling, though it appears to be invisible, hence, made of glass. The pervasiveness of this inequity is everywhere. Men are still assumed to be the head of the household if a woman applies for a bank loan. It took years and a joint resolution by several professional organizations just to get the use of "he" discussed as a generic reference in writing. Social practices are systems of meaning at work in society, some of which may operate below the level of consciousness. Unpacking the social practices that perpetuate forces like gender inequity is what disrupting the commonplace is about.

As Westheimer and Kahne have pointed out, for the most part, we respond to the surface structure of issues rather than to the deep structure. Rather than taking collective action and examining what forces are in play that make hunger an issue (in one of the richest societies in the world, we might add), we react at the surface level by contributing to a food drive. To be critically literate is to unpack the issue; to bring to conscious awareness the forces that are at play; to realize that hunger, poverty, and race overlap; and to conclude that in order to eliminate hunger one has to eliminate both poverty and racism. In addition to collecting food, the critically literate citizen might respond by working with governmental agencies to understand and improve local employment opportunities. This can include working to bring new businesses into the community, knowing that with new businesses come more employment opportunities and the hope of a long-term solution to hunger for some people in the community. All of these suggestions disrupt our commonplace notions of how to respond to the problem of hunger.

Another disrupting idea that teachers and students need to understand is that no text is neutral. Colin Lankshear (1997) and Janks (2010) argue that critical literacy is first and foremost about language and power. Barbara Comber (2001) argues that students in the 21st century need to understand the kind of work texts do and how they do this work. What these and many other authors call for is a particular kind of language study—a language study that interrogates texts in terms of what "frames" (Lakoff, 2004) or "cultural models" (Gee, 1996) are used to position readers in particular ways and endow them with particular identities. Lakoff defines frames as "mental structures that shape the way we see the world … the goals we seek, the plans we make, the way we act" (p. xv). Shannon (1995), in seeking to move beyond commonplace understandings, argues for the development of a language of critique. Gee (1999) wants us to understand how language shapes identity, and how words, grammar, and cultural discourses work in terms of agency, passivity, and power. If we return to the Westheimer and Kahne example of citizenship and hunger, it makes a significant difference if participants see hunger from the frames of poverty and collective responsibility rather than from the frames of racism and individual volunteerism.

Gunter Kress (2003) argues that in this new media age the screen is overtaking the page in terms of its ability to communicate. To the extent this is true, the texts we use to help students disrupt their commonplace beliefs are semiotic, involving multiple signs systems. An advertisement, for example, often contains written language, a provocative picture, and without doubt, a social intent or function. These elements come together to create a text that represents some socially valued practice that is meant to convince people to buy into a social practice or way of thinking. Seeing ads as texts in this way focuses attention on the definition of literacy in operation, the social practices sustaining that definition, and the pragmatic effects of that definition as read by others.

In a recent study, Albers, Harste, Vander-Zanden and Felderman (2008) found that while pre-service teachers and fifth graders were good at reading individual signs in ads, neither group had much success in identifying the underlying tacit messages, many of which were extremely problematic from a critical literacy perspective (Albers et al., 2008). In the study, pre-service teachers and fifth grade students were shown a Wal-Mart ad introducing a new Barbie clothing collection for girls. The ad shows three smiling girls dressed in various shades of pink clothing (skirts, tops, stockings) as they march confidently down a fashion runway. In the margins of the ad there are images of Barbie dolls and accessories that complement the outfits being worn by the girls. When reading this ad, the pre-service teachers said nothing critical about Barbie, the color scheme of the clothing line, or the anchored images of Wal-Mart and Barbie in the margins of the ad. Their responses were descriptive: *Beautiful little girls*; *Pretty like Barbie*; *Stylish, pink, walking down the runway like models*; *Showing girls and the dolls in a high style fashion show*; *Portraying the kids as fashion runway models, just like if you wore these clothes, you could be a model too.* The use of such general descriptors of value indicates the extent to which viewers of these ads participated and identified with the lifestyle presented in the context of these ads. The designers of this ad were selling not only a product, but a lifestyle—children dressed according to specific standards of what is supposed to look good confidently marching on a runway—which they hope children and adults will see as something they want to buy into. The pre-service teachers identified and engaged with the discourses of affluence, happiness, and fashion. Fifth graders identified with the physical elements of the ads such as the setting and the clothes being worn. Neither group attempted to unpack the bigger messages these individual elements were working together to send.

REFLECTION POINT 2.2

Possible Interpretations

What are some possible interpretations regarding why the pre-service teachers and the fifth graders did not unpack the bigger underlying messages in the ad?

Interrogating Multiple Perspectives

Being a critically literate citizen involves both inquiry and interrogation of our beliefs and actions. Seeing education as inquiry goes well beyond a rejection of the idea that knowledge is something one passively receives. Education as inquiry means that as learners and as critical citizens we must participate in ongoing knowledge production and generation. To be a literate citizen is to be an inquirer who interrogates multiple perspectives and is willing to take a stance based on personal involvement and understanding. Gordon Wells (1999) defines inquiry-based learning as taking place through a continuing spiral of knowing: "Over time, current understandings derived from past experiences are tested, critiqued and enhanced through engagement with new information in the course of action and dialogic knowledge building" (p. 25). To be a critical inquirer is to be collaborative, constantly examining what one knows from multiple perspectives. We often equate being educated with being open-minded enough to see issues from different sides. Westheimer and Kahne (2004) point out that "justice-oriented students must develop the ability to communicate with and learn from those who hold different perspectives" (p. 243). But they also explain how "educating justice-oriented citizens requires that they be prepared to effectively promote their goals as individuals and groups in sometimes-contentious political arenas" (p. 243). So, while being open to alternate perspectives is important, it does not follow that all perspectives are equal. In fact some perspectives are often privileged or dominant while others are marginalized.

In some ways, multiple perspectives provide us with a self-correction strategy. By seriously considering different points of view and how such points of view advantage and disadvantage, we can metaphorically see around corners for purposes of identifying problematic arguments. This strategy works best over time. While competing perspectives may seem equally valid when first proposed, over the long haul some perspectives will prove to be more robust or to have more explanatory power. Some take on increased significance as we continue to learn more and think more deeply about issues. An example is Wayne Booth's insight (1988) that literacy and "ultimate readings" (p. xiii) are finally always a matter of ethics. By this he means that whatever meaning we finally arrive at has embedded in it a set of values and, as readers, must take responsibility for these values and the conclusions we reach because of their existence. While everyone may have a right to his or her own opinion, multiple perspectives invite people to continue to grapple with fundamental issues, thus disrupting our tendency to provide easy answers to complex problems.

A good example of a theory that is built on a belief in the importance of multiple perspectives is Luke and Freebody's four resources model of reading. In their seminal 1997 article, the authors described four "necessary but not sufficient 'roles' for the reader in a postmodern, text-based culture" (p. 47). These roles focused on the reader as a code breaker, a meaning maker, a text user, and a text critic. At the time, Luke and Freebody's focus on readers as text users and text critics provided an exciting new perspective since existing theories had little to say about readers as text users or critics. But what was also so important about this model was its conscious denial of a "single definitive, truthful, scientific, universally effective, or culturally appropriate way of teaching or even defining literacy" (pp. 47–48).

REFLECTION POINT 2.3

Multiple Perspectives

Think about an issue, topic or incident that you have been grappling with or that has perplexed you recently.

- What are three possible perspectives you could have taken to better understand the issue or topic?
- How might each of the three perspectives help you to think differently about the issue or topic?

Unpacking Issues Socio-politically

Few of us got into teaching to fight for our political rights or the political rights of others. The arrival of federal legislation directed at literacy instruction, including how it must be taught, has forced educators to become much more aware of how political the literacy teaching really is. This realization echoes Westheimer and Kahne's (2004) assertion that justice-oriented educators understand how "effective democratic citizens need opportunities to analyze and understand the interplay of social, economic, and political forces" (p. 242).

Taking a critical perspective requires a conscious awareness of language and how it works in powerful ways. Hillary Janks (2000) argues that it is important for teachers to redesign education by disrupting how language is currently being used to maintain dominant ways of thinking, by exploring about how one might create spaces for non-dominant groups to gain access to powerful discourses without devaluing their own language and culture, and by advocating for diversity as a cultural resource. For example, gender stereotypes like "girls should be pretty" are embedded into many everyday texts (like the Barbie ad discussed earlier). Janks (2010) describes how an advertisement for fruit juice took a totally different form depending on the gender of the person in the ad. When men were featured, the message was that drinking the juice enhanced their energy and ability to compete in a sport. When images of women were used to sell the product, the women were constructed as pretty to look at but passive and powerless. Providing opportunities for students to explore how texts like these ads characterize gender and function to shape society is what Janks advocates in terms of re-designing education.

Similarly, Colin Lankshear and Peter McLaren (1993) argue that teachers need to adopt a critical perspective—one that challenges the legitimacy of unequal power relationships, questions existing hierarchies, and re-examines social structures that keep power in the hands of a few. Critical educators interrogate privilege and status (not just in the lives of others but in their own lives as well), investigate oppression (especially forms of oppression that appear to be natural or a part of the status quo), and use resistance, dialogue, and public debate as tools to engage in the politics of daily life (Fairclough, 1989; Hinchey, 1998). Students are invited to study a wide range of power relationships, from why some children are being marginalized in their own school to why some groups are being marginalized in the immediate and larger community. Through such investigations participants gain an understanding of how language works to maintain power relationships as well as an understanding of how language might be used to disrupt the status quo for the purpose of achieving a more equitable and just world.

If we go back to Westheimer and Kahne, we need to ask ourselves: How does our need for "more" contribute to making hunger a community and global issue? In the big scheme of things, recycling plastic and changing one's light bulbs might be tokenistic at best. Have we Americans tacitly accepted a throwaway society that consumes a disproportionate share of the world's resources? In the aftermath of the 9/11 attacks, President Bush appeared on television not to talk about how our political practices have angered the Middle East and why we need to position ourselves differently, but to encourage Americans to get in their cars and go shopping! Our society is built on consumption and spending. Our need for more fuels the economy but also creates two distinct classes: the "haves" and the "have-nots." Unpacking the socio-political is often difficult and involves making inferences and connections between things that are not immediately obvious. "Thinking Green," for example, is going to have to become connected to our use of resources (not just replacing one light bulb for another type) if we are to become critically literate about hunger and see its connection to global warming.

Barbara Kamler (2001) makes the curricular case that in addressing socio-political issues it is easier to start locally and then think globally. She uses her writing program as a way to get difficult social issues out into the open. She begins by asking students to write personal narratives about their lives. After revising, editing, and publishing these pieces, she celebrates their writing by having students identify what larger social forces were in play that gave rise to their personal tales. So, for example, if a student brought up a memory about how she was bullied on the playground, Kamler would help her to identify the social and political forces that were at play. Depending on the writer's narrative and how the bullying episode transpired, she might focus on the discourse that males are supposed to be tough; that "real men" (and boys) stand up for their rights; or that women and girls ought to know their place and get out of the way. Of course there are also national and global policies that support the socio-political experiences of females being bullied. As of this writing, we have yet to have a female president of the USA; most religious groups position women in servile roles; and boy babies, (worldwide), are preferred by new parents over girl babies. In the play, *Fiddler on the Roof* (Stein, Bock, & Harnick, 2004), Perchik, the political activist, asks Hodel to marry him. Sheldon Harnick, the lyricist, has these two characters make the point that everything, every topic—and even marriage itself—is political:

Perchik:	There's a question… A certain question I want to discuss with you.
Hodel:	Yes?
Perchik:	It's a political question.
Hodel:	What is it?
Perchik:	The question of…marriage.
Hodel:	Is this a political question?
Perchik:	Well, yes. Yes, everything's political. Like everything else, the relationship between a man and a woman has a socioeconomic base. Marriage must be founded on mutual beliefs. A common attitude and philosophy towards society…
Hodel:	—And affection?
Perchik:	Well, yes, of course. That is also necessary. Such a relationship can have positive social values. When two people face the world with unity and solidarity…
Hodel:	And affection?
Perchik:	Yes, that is an important element! At any rate, I… I personally am in favour of such a socioeconomic relationship.
Hodel:	I think…you are asking me to marry you.
Perchik:	Well…in a theoretical sense…yes. I am.
Hodel:	I was hoping you were.

While humorous, this segment makes the point that everything is political in that people have interests and goals that are not the same. While Hodel keeps pushing her agenda for marriage to be built on love and affection, Perchik sidesteps this idea and keeps going back to what is more important in his view—economic and political factors. Marriage (between a man and a woman) is often just assumed and is not interrogated in terms of the underlying tensions that the exchange between Perchik and Hodel demonstrates. When marriage involves members of the same sex, the tensions become even more visible, and more often than not, socially and politically divisive.

Dennis Sumara and Brent Davis (1999) make the argument that curriculum should be designed to help students identify and then question what is considered to be "normal" or the status quo. They see questioning the normative as a way of opening up the curriculum to conversation. In terms of the writing curriculum, they might ask students to write an alternative narrative to the one that they first wrote for Barbara Kamler. They would argue that by getting students to focus on the non-normative, the socio-political forces at play become salient. Cochran-Smith and Lytle (1999) reported using a similar strategy in their teacher researcher courses by asking students to write about a time when school failed them. By focusing on what went wrong, the socio-political forces at work become clear and the ensuing discussion can focus on social action, or what can be done.

TRY THIS: Pedagogical Strategy 2.1

A Time When School Failed You

Have your students do a free-write on a time when school failed them. Following are some focusing questions for them to consider.

- What happened?
- Who were the key players involved in the incident?
- Who failed you? How?
- What language and actions led to your feeling of failure?
- How did you react then? How did you feel you were positioned?
- What might you do differently now? How might you position yourself differently?

Taking Social Action

Taking social action is an attempt to move the school curriculum to the community; to make it relevant to the lives of the students we teach. Sometimes it is difficult to think about what kind of social action to take. If we go back to the Westheimer and Kahne example of citizenship and hunger, for example, it is hard to envision a group of second graders marching on city hall demanding that the poor be given jobs and health care. This option ought not be ruled out, however, as it may be quite effective. Shelley Harwayne (1999) reported that the second graders in her school in New York City adopted a homeless man and made sure that he was fed each and every day for the year. They also found him a place to stay (where he was dry and relatively safe), a job sweeping the sidewalk in front of one of the stores on the street, and learned a whole lot about the complexity of homelessness and what would be needed in order to make it go away. Where this action may not have gone far enough is in engaging in a conversation regarding the privileges through which the children were able to engage in such social action.

While critical theorists are interested in what counts as literacy in a society, they are even more interested in what social practices are in place. They argue that in order to change what counts as literacy, the social practices—the practices that give certain forms of literacy more clout than other forms—need to change. And the Discourses that keep these social practices in place need to change also. If these larger social practices don't change, then no real change has occurred. This argument is based on research suggesting that schools for working-class children are very different from schools for children coming from affluent neighborhoods (Anyon, 1997; Finn, 1999). Although the general topics covered in these schools may be the same, the level of engagement by teachers and pupils differs dramatically. Too often, the social practices of working-class schools prepare students for labor that is mechanical and routine. The social practices of schools located in affluent neighborhoods, on the other hand, prepare students for work as artists, intellectuals, legal and scientific experts, and other professional roles that involve creativity, are intrinsically satisfying and are rewarded with social power and high salaries. The children's capacity for creativity and planning in working-class schools is often denied or ignored, while at the same time the children's capacity for creativity and planning in affluent neighborhoods is encouraged (Anyon, 1997). While social practices shape many things (including who gets what kind of schooling), they also influence which methods get used in which schools and with which students.

Confronting these larger systems of meaning is not easy. Nonetheless, one way to think about critical social practices in the classroom is to think about what this means in terms of using language and other sign systems to get things done in the world. By making a decision to use critical social practices, teachers create spaces that have the potential for students to disrupt what is considered to be normal. This happens when students are invited to ask new questions, see everyday issues through new lenses, demystify naturalized views of the world, and visualize how things might be different (Giroux, 1994). Critical social practices support students in gaining a greater understanding of how social and cultural forces shape their choices and their lives.

Freire (1970) calls for us to encourage our students to be actors rather than spectators in the world. He stresses the importance of reflection followed by the kind of action that can transform the world. Agency is strengthened when students compose their own narratives, counter-narratives, letters, essays, reports, poems, commercials, posters, plays, podcasts (Vasquez, 2005) and web pages to promote social change. They participate in discussions that focus on issues of oppression, fairness, and transformation. They use a variety of litera-cies to conduct surveys and gather data to explain, expose, and find solutions for real-world problems (Vasquez & Felderman, 2013; Vasquez, 2005; Hinchley, 1998). They understand how art works to position viewers as well as endow them with an identity they may or may not wish to take on. In similar fashion they use the arts to express critical understandings and to get messages of jus-tice and democracy out into the world. Instead of being positioned as helpless victims, students use critical social practices to rewrite their identities as social activists who challenge the status quo and demand change (Leland & Harste, 2000; Altwerger & Strauss, 2002; Flores, Cousin, & Diaz, 1991). They use cul-tural resources and critical literacies to develop powerful voices and to speak out collectively against injustice.

Pat Thomson's notion of the "virtual school bag" (2002) provides a useful exam-ple for how teachers can take social action. Drawing on Pierre Bourdieu's (1986) notion of cultural capital and Luis Moll's notion of funds of knowledge (1992), Thomson describes how all children enter school with a virtual school bag full of the things they've learned at home including their language(s), abilities, and past experiences. Once in school, however, some students' experiences are more valued and their school bags are metaphorically opened more frequently—while other children are rarely allowed to use the cultural resources they've acquired at home.

TRY THIS: Pedagogical Strategy 2.2

Unpacking the Virtual Schoolbag

Peggy McIntosh's piece on white privilege (1989) is a good example of reflexivity in action. She begins by saying "I have come to see white privilege as an invisible package of unearned assets that I can count on cashing in each day, but about which I was 'meant' to remain oblivious." She then goes on to say that this awareness makes her "newly accountable" in that she must now ask what she will "do to lessen or end it" (p. 1).

Unpack your own virtual schoolbag and ask your students to unpack theirs. In doing so consider the following:

- What are some of the positions of privilege from which you speak or act?
- In what spaces and places do such privileges advantage you?

- Does this advantage sometimes come at the expense of others?
- What difference would it make for you to know the privileges that you carry in your virtual schoolbag?
- What might you do with what you know?
- How might what you learn about yourself help you to become a more informed and reflective teacher?

Understanding One's Own Involvement

Critical literacy is not just a subject we want added to the curriculum. While on one level critical literacy might be thought of as an academic subject, it really is a lot more. It involves action, starting with one's self. We see critical literacy as fundamentally a call to action; a call to position oneself differently in the world, a call to take seriously the relationship between language and power as noted by Janks (2010), as well as to take seriously the relationship between other semiotic systems and power.

As Edelsky (1999) sees it, critically literate citizens will not only talk differently but will live differently as well. To go back to the Westheimer and Kahne example, when studying hunger, for example, it isn't good enough to point out the wasteful practices of others, or even map out and understand the complexities of how discrimination fuels poverty and hunger. In addition, we also have to be able to see how the practices we personally engage in perpetuate racism, poverty, and hunger. Most of America, for example, lives in neighborhoods where their neighbors look, act, and believe pretty much as they do. This means that poor people tend to live with poor people and rich people tend to live alongside other rich people. Our housing practices do little to help. While gated communities may advertise themselves as open to everyone, in reality only people making a certain amount of money can afford to live in these enclaves. Our failure to protest segregated housing practices means that we become part of the problem rather than part of the solution. The systems of meaning that have always discriminated against the poor remain in place. So, by not acting, we really *are* acting, but not in a critically literate way.

Metaphorically, we see understanding one's own involvement in an issue as the ability to catch oneself with one's hand in the cookie jar (Leland & Harste, 2000). Scholars have referred to this ability as "reflexivity" (Peirce, 1931–58; Eco, 1970) and have defined it as an awareness of one's personal complicity in maintaining the status quo (or the very systems of injustice one is fighting against). Even though we may be committed to social change, more often than not, we are part of the dominant culture and hence, part of the problem. Until we understand how our current identity and the positions we take mitigate our reform efforts, we cannot truly become part of the solution.

Another way to understand reflexivity is through re-naming or re-theorizing. As Freire (1970) points out, "once named the world in turn reappears to the namers as a problem and requires of them a new naming" (p. 76). Notice that Freire uses the word "namers." Naming and re-naming are social activities; they happen in dialogue and debate with others. This re-naming cycle involves re-theorizing—questioning our assumptions about how the world works and, if necessary, changing our beliefs. hooks (1994) sees changing beliefs as a first step in taking action when she argues for "theory as intervention" and theory "as a way to challenge the status quo" (p. 60). Freire calls this "praxis." He sees reflection and action as cornerstones of reflexivity.

While we define reflexivity as using oneself and others to outgrow one's current beliefs, in operation reflexivity means that there is no claiming of the moral ground. To be critically literate is to develop eyes in the back of your head that can watch you make change while at the same time interrogate how you, as an active participant in your community, are part of the very problem you are trying to solve. Peggy McIntosh's piece on white privilege (1989) is a good example of reflexivity in action. She begins by saying "I have come to see white privilege as an invisible package of unearned assets that I can count on cashing in each day, but about which I was 'meant' to remain oblivious." She then goes on to say that this awareness makes her "newly accountable" in that she must now ask what she will "do to lessen or end it" (p. 1).

Towards a More Critically Literate Citizenry for the 21st Century

Critical literacies are rooted in principles of democracy and justice, of questioning and analysis, of resistance and action (Edelsky, 1999)—all uncommon in traditional pedagogies that define a teacher as a transmitter of knowledge. It is interesting that even though democratic principles are highly touted in textbooks and political rhetoric, they are not frequently taken up in classroom routines (Giroux, 1994). We suspect that one of the reasons for this is our tendency to develop curriculum from memory rather than from engagement. We see developing curriculum from memory as making decisions based on what we taught the previous year, on what we think is fundamental to know in a discipline, on what we perceive as mandated curricular frameworks, or even on the focus of the basic textbook in an area. The problem with these sources is that they position our students as consumers rather than participants in education. Students come to understand knowledge as a set of facts to be learned rather than as a personal investment in understanding and transforming their world. An alternative is to build curriculum based on what we know about language learning while keeping a critical focus on everything we do. Following is a beginning set of principles that might guide curriculum as we go about developing a more critically literate citizenry for the 21st century.

- All students come to school with diverse cultural, linguistic, and experiential resources and literacies. As teachers it behooves us to make use of these resources as an integral part of our teaching practice by building curriculum that respects and builds on these.
- We need to understand and name the social practices we currently support in order to re-think what social practices best support our students. What social practices we support in the classroom affect what counts as literacy and ultimately the kind of literate beings we produce.
- Teachers who actively engage in critical literacies are more likely to have students who are more reflexive, consciously engaged, and students who take on alternate ways of being, as well as take responsibility for inquiring into issues of importance to them. Here within lies the challenge of teacher education and the preparation of pre-service and in-service teachers for the 21st century.

Paulo Freire (1970) probably said it best when he noted that education is never neutral. It either liberates, domesticates, or alienates. Carole Edelsky (1999) talks about the necessity of understanding that a teacher's approach to classroom literacy can never be politically neutral. Literacy can be taught as a tool of critical inquiry or of passive transmission. It can be a vehicle for posing and solving important social problems or for accepting official explanations and solutions (pp. 121–123). Negotiating critical literacies and living a critically literate life means delving into risky topics that surround children's lives. It is not enough to treat critical literacy as a topic of conversation; we have to go out and do something as well. We have to embody critical literacies: "One imperative of a critical pedagogy is to offer students opportunities to become aware of their potential and deepen democratic values, institutions, and identities" (Giroux & Giroux, 2004, p. 84). While Barbara Kamler (2001) focuses on writing, her advice can be read as calling for living a critically literate curriculum: "it is through the process of designing that writers [and we add, 'future citizens'] produce new representations of reality and at the same time remake themselves ..." (p. 54).

RESOURCE BOX 2.1

Resources on Critical Literacy

Comber, B. & Simpson, A. (2001). *Negotiating critical literacies in classrooms.* New York, NY: Routledge.

Cooper, K. & White, R.E. (Eds.) (2008). *Critical literacies in action: Social perspectives and teaching practices*. New York, NY: Sense.

Dozier, C., Johnston, P., & Rogers, R. (2005). *Critical literacy/Critical teaching*. New York, NY: Teachers College Press.

Janks, H. (2010). *Literacy and power*. New York, NY : Routledge.

Lewison, M., Leland, C., & Harste, J.C. (2008). *Creating critical classrooms*. Mahwah, NJ: Lawrence Erlbaum.

Morgan, W. (1997). *Critical literacy in the classroom: The art of the possible*. London, UK: Routledge.

Vasquez, V. (2004). *Negotiating critical literacy with young children*. New York, NY: Routledge.

Vasquez, V. (2010). *Getting beyond I like the book: Creating spaces for critical literacy in K-6 settings*. Newark, DE: International Reading Association.

Vasquez, V. & Felderman, C. (2013). *Technology and critical literacy in early childhood*. New York, NY: Routledge.

3

OUTGROWING OUR CURRENT SELVES: IT'S NOT JUST A JOB— IT'S A LIFESTYLE

There is no greater research project than ourselves ...

(Frank, 2010)

For several years Stacie has asked her pre-service teachers to consider their motivation for teaching. In doing so she has them examine their underlying personal orientations and assumptions by having them write a teaching philosophy paper. In the fall of 2007, one of her pre-service teachers challenged this assignment. "Shouldn't my job be about teaching and . . . not about my own personal feelings towards what I teach?", he asked. Stacie's argument for giving the teaching philosophy assignment is that effective classroom teachers need to understand the reasoning behind the choices they make. Her student's statement helped her realize that perhaps teachers do not truly understand that many of the choices they make in the classroom are based on a combination of personal and theoretical knowledge and experience.

bell hooks (1994) argues that the self-actualized teacher connects who they are to the lives of their students and they understand what they teach is deeply connected to who they are. However, there exists a commonly held belief, just as Stacie's student articulated, that a teacher's pedagogical practice should be separate from their personal lives. According to Bartolome (2003), the focus on the practical often occurs when teachers do not examine their own assumptions, values, and beliefs. From a critical literacy perspective examining one's own assumptions, values, and beliefs is part and parcel of understanding the position(s) from which we speak, the position(s) from which we teach and the Discourses (ways of being, doing, acting, talking, and thinking) that shape those positionings.

This chapter examines how the development and use of a teaching philosophy can help educators unpack their Discursive practices and the ideological positions through which they engage in the practice of teaching. These of course are the same positions through which they interpret their students' learning. This chapter also considers the following.

- What it means to outgrow our current self.
- Why it is important to examine and understand how we are positioned.
- What steps we need to consider in order to outgrow the ideas and philoso-phies that prevent us from truly actualizing a practice of critical literacy both inside and outside of the classroom.

In this chapter, we focus on one high school teacher in an urban setting and identify core practices in the development and enactment of his teaching philosophy. The core practices examined are the pedagogical and theoretical knowledge that guide this teacher in the development of his teaching philosophy and bell hooks' (1994) notion of the self-actualized teacher and how this theory functions in terms of the enactment of his beliefs and how it helped him to outgrow his current self.

What is a Teaching Philosophy?

Many teacher education programs and professional development workshops incorporate assignments, activities, or discussions regarding one's teaching phi-losophy. Often the intent is for participants to develop a viewpoint about the practical and theoretical characteristics of education. According to Hansen (2007), a philosophy of education is comprised of (1) a statement of values, (2) a moral compass and (3) an abiding engine of ideas. Hansen believes a philosophy reflects what a thinker esteems (p. 7). More importantly, Hansen argues that the philoso-phy statement assists in examining the unexamined noting that in the absence of such a statement, "the teacher would have no recourse but to rely on unexamined habits; on memories of his or her own teachers, as well as experiences as a student; and on resources contrived by other people whose outlook may or may not be compatible, much less more enlightened than the teacher's own" (p. 8). A philosophy statement therefore offers perspective, which comes from framing teaching using particular Discursive practices.

Robert Peterson in his 2003 article "Teaching how to read the world and change it: Critical pedagogy in the intermediate grades" examined how he became a proponent of the Freireian perspective on teaching. He argued that after he read philosopher Paulo Freire's work, teaching and learning became more than just "relevant" and "student centered" (p. 365). He realized in order to make a differ-ence in his bi-lingual inner-city classroom, he needed to incorporate the Freireian method of "problem posing" education. This method required that he and his stu-dents become actors in figuring out the world through a process of mutual com-munication (p. 366). However, what is unique about this teacher's change is that he realized that the "Freireian Method" was not just about his practical experiences in the classroom, but it focused on him changing how he saw his students. He realized that "one has to have a perspective about learners and learning which runs counter to the dominant educational ideology" (p. 366). His philosophy about teaching and learning became one through which he embraced the experiences of his students and respected their cultures, languages, and dialects (p. 366).

Hansen (2007) believes that teachers who operate without knowledge of their philosophy have only one recourse—they must rely on "unexamined habits" (p. 8). The question that remains is whether or not a philosophy of education does change a teacher's pedagogy.

Outgrowing Our Current Selves

We have come to realize that while we have a vested interest in making sure students achieve, something more powerful is in the idea that our interests may be inextricably linked to our personal histories and therefore how these histories position us in our classrooms. For example, Sullivan (1996) articulates this fact through the notion of self-reflexivity. She states:

> Our field of inquiry is quite often academe itself: we undertake fieldwork in university classrooms and teachers' lunchrooms, and our informants are often students or other teachers. When studying literacy and pedagogy in such contexts, it is easy to forget that our own status as researchers, as academics, is itself a social location invested with diverse and contestable meanings. If our status is presumed as a given at the outset of study rather than as a formation in relationship to an other, we may miss opportunities to learn how we are being constructed and the effects such constructions have on other literacies we then "uncover".
>
> *(pp. 106–107)*

How can we not consider how our own theoretical and political assumptions and beliefs become a part of the work that we do as teachers? While many researchers argue for objectivity and detachment, researchers like Chiseri-Strater (1996) see a need for an examination of the self in order to "reveal what a researcher was positioned to see, to know, and to understand" (p. 123). She goes on to articulate that an omission of the self may hide the many conflicts that teachers and researchers face. More importantly she states, "the only direct way for a reader to obtain information about how positioning affects methodology is for the researcher to write about it" (p.123). How do we come to name and understand our own position and how we are being positioned by others? We believe it starts with theory. We believe that theory and practice are inextricably linked as noted by Lewin (1952) "there is nothing more practical than a good theory" (p. 169). However, we also believe that theory must be actualized. This is the way we believe teachers can outgrow old notions and beliefs that do not serve to promote a critical literacy framework. Theorized ideas mean nothing unless you are able to live out those theories in real life as a philosophy that guides how you see yourself and others.

Theory and Practice: You Can't Have One Without the Other

How is it that a philosophy can guide a teacher's pedagogy? What theoretical knowledge is necessary and how is this understanding enacted in a classroom? In 2004, Stacie conducted a yearlong ethnographic study of a high school English teacher at Southwest High School in south Los Angeles, California. Southwest High School is located in south Los Angles in a multiethnic community with about a half-million residents. The teacher, Cruz, had taught English at Southwest for six years and was himself a student of the Los Angeles public schools. After spending a year with this English teacher and his eleventh and twelfth grade students, she came to understand how a teacher develops and enacts a philosophy about teaching.

D-4 was the name given to Cruz's classroom bungalow that sat behind the main Southwest High School building. The outside didn't seem out of the ordinary. In fact, it looked the same as the rest of the classrooms that sat behind the high school. Even the inside seemed ordinary. Posters were mounted on the walls and the classroom was in a fairly traditional set-up. However, these posters were not ordinary in any way. These posters spoke of revolution and political action. Three posters in particular caught Stacie's attention; Talib Kweli a rapper, Erika Badu a neo-soul singer, and Che Guevara the revolutionary. The Guevara poster had on it the following text: "When I give food to the poor they call me a saint. When I ask why the poor have no food they call me a communist." This teacher's classroom space offered one glimpse into his philosophy.

Cruz had a strong foundation informing who he wanted to be as a teacher. This foundation was shaped through his earlier experiences as a student within the Los Angeles public schools and his exposure to different educational philosophies as a graduate student. Just as many theorists discuss how teachers rely on "unexamined habits" (Hansen, 2007) and "earlier impressions, ideas and orientations" (Lortie, 1975), Cruz discussed how his earlier notions about teaching guided his philosophy.

> [I always wanted to] be that type of teacher I wish I always had. [I wanted a teacher] who helped me understand my reality in ways that Paulo Freire talks about. I didn't know about Paulo Freire at the time. I wish [I had] somebody who understood and knew the conditions of the community especially the way that we felt.

Cruz highlights two key ideas. First, he realized that he wanted to become "that type of teacher I wish I always had." He realized there were things about his own education that were lacking and that many of his teachers never understood him or the needs of his community. Second, he considered philosopher Paulo Freire as key to understanding the kind of teacher he wanted to be. Freire, a Brazilian educator, challenged the conditions of living in Brazil, which oppressed some while privileging others, with what he called "a pedagogy for the oppressed." This pedagogy provided a revolutionary way to create a school grounded in a new educational praxis. Freire's work required that questions be asked of power, culture and oppression. For Freire, education was about social agency, voice, and participation in the democratic system. Paulo Freire was a key theorist for Cruz and his philosophy as noted when he wrote the following.

> *I think when it comes down to it; critical pedagogy is really about the distribution of power. It's about the powerful and the powerless. And when someone is critical, they understand how history is always present in the moment. And by understanding that, [we] recognize the privilege that certain histories have over others and [we] work to decentralize people's privilege and make it more inclusive to those that are usually marginalized. I don't mean that in an abstract sense I actually mean that in an economic, cultural and political sense. So critical pedagogy in many ways is trying to seek out what is not there and always questioning what we assume to be true. [We have to] be more inclusive of those who don't have voices and ultimately rethink and redistribute who has power.*

The previous thoughts from Cruz, exemplifies a core principle regarding his understanding of the role of theory, in this case, critical pedagogy. Additionally, while sharing his thoughts he revealed crucial tenets central to his pedagogy. Cruz articulated what he knew and how he acquired the knowledge that ultimately drove his teaching. However, how was this philosophy enacted in his classroom?

Prior to the first day of class, Stacie asked Cruz to further discuss how he enacted what he believed about Paulo Freire in his classroom. He responded stating:

> *Like television, music, and films were infiltrated by marginalized folks, we're [teachers] slowly taking over education. Everything I hope to look at focuses on progressively transforming Southwest High School and serving the needs of our students. Basically, trying to re-think a school-wide curriculum working towards self and social change.*

Additionally Cruz sent Stacie his course syllabus, which he interpreted as being his first step at implementing Paulo Freire's philosophy in his classroom. After looking at his syllabus, the first thing she noticed in bold letters was the D-4 core responsibilities (refer to Figure 3.1).

According to Cruz, each "responsibility" is a glimpse into how he enacted his philosophy in his classroom. Cruz saw the first responsibility as an example of Paulo Freire's theoretical idea of critical pedagogy. "Have each other's back," according to Cruz, displayed a unique language that was both familiar and

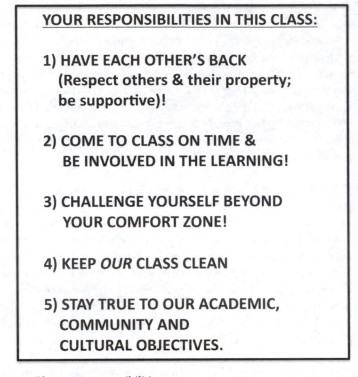

YOUR RESPONSIBILITIES IN THIS CLASS:

1) HAVE EACH OTHER'S BACK
(Respect others & their property;
be supportive)!

2) COME TO CLASS ON TIME &
BE INVOLVED IN THE LEARNING!

3) CHALLENGE YOURSELF BEYOND
YOUR COMFORT ZONE!

4) KEEP *OUR* CLASS CLEAN

5) STAY TRUE TO OUR ACADEMIC,
COMMUNITY AND
CULTURAL OBJECTIVES.

FIGURE 3.1 Classroom responsibilities.

comforting to the students but also displayed Freire's notion of solidarity, social responsibility and discipline (Freire, 1970, p. 156). Another responsibility pointed out by Cruz was "challenging yourself beyond your comfort zone." Cruz believed that this rule spoke to Freire's idea of challenging the status quo in an effort to discover alternative paths for self and social development (Freire, 1970, p. 156). He felt that within his classroom it was important for his students to think outside the box. Finally with the last rule, Cruz introduced the core meaning of his class. The idea of staying true to academics, community, and cultural objectives became the central focus of his classroom. Through this last responsibility Cruz wanted to provide a lens for connecting what students learn to who they are.

Through "classroom responsibilities," Cruz revealed what he believed about education. What he esteems about Paulo Freire was not just empty sayings; he brought Freireian tenets to fruition through his "classroom responsibilities." His philosophy about education is comprised of a statement of values, a moral compass and an abiding engine of ideas, all the essential components that Hansen (2007) believes should be a part of a teacher's philosophy. However, the final piece to developing his philosophy was not just how he enacted his philosophy in his classroom but how he was able to "examine the unexamined" (p. 8).

REFLECTION POINT 3.1

Analyzing Signs and Posters

Take a look around your classroom or someone else's classroom.

- What sorts of posters or signs do you see on the walls?
- What do those texts tell you about the teacher's theoretical orientation(s)?

Here are some questions you can ask:

- Who is advantaged by those signs?
- What kind of work do the signs accomplish in the classroom?
- How do the signs position the teacher?, students?, others? (Who are these others?)

FIGURE 3.2 Class poster.

TRY THIS: Pedagogical Strategy 3.1

Re-designing Dominant School Posters

The image in Figure 3.2 is a poster created by an in-service teacher to replace the more dominant types of posters found on many school walls such as "If you are walking you are not talking" and so forth. The poster counters this sort of dominant practice through its message "ask questions" and "speak out".

As a follow up to Reflection Point 3.1 think about, talk about and then create counter-narrative posters that disrupt problematic ones that you may have encountered.

The Self-actualized Teacher: What We Teach is Who We Are

The idea of self-actualization presents many possibilities for teaching. According to hooks (1994), teachers who are self-actualized are able to teach in a manner that empowers students and moves beyond the boundaries of compartmentalized bits of knowledge and narrowed perspectives. hooks (1994) believes that teaching can become a career that engages not only the student, but the teacher as well. As mentioned earlier, when teachers are self-actualized they consider teaching as a practice of understanding students and themselves. Cruz is a teacher who we believe is self-actualized.

He talked to Stacie about how he was a student of the Los Angeles Unified School District and how by the tenth grade he dropped out of high school. He explained that his attitude about school was like many of the students he taught and he understood the positions of many of his students who were on the verge of dropping out. Often in his class he reminds his students, "Don't punk out now. I've been where you are and I know how hard it is." His narrative also included how he got his GED, graduated from a state university, and eventually went on to teach high school. Additionally, through his narrative he articulated what teaching means to him.

> This is not a job to me; it's a life style. It's not something I do and not go home and think about. It's something I do that makes me- me. And none of it ever feels like work because it's just what I do. I know that I'm not doing it for me. Then when I'm tired and I don't want to do an assignment, I think of some of my former students and I know that I need to work hard and not [just] for me. It's not something we can wait to happen, it's something we have to make happen. And I don't care what color you are. I don't care where you come from. You can be a critical pedagogue, but part of that responsibility means reflecting every day through theory about your practice. Make adjustments. Make critical adjustments to your practice.

Cruz demonstrated how he is self-actualized, how he lives the theories that shape his ideological beliefs. He admitted that change happened for him because of his ongoing negotiation of his teaching. Cruz's statement spoke to the purpose of an educational philosophy as a perspective on a profession that is not just a job, but a lifestyle. He realized that in order for students to reach their academic goals, he had to unpack his Discursive practices and understand the ideological positions he held about education.

TRY THIS: Pedagogical Strategy 3.2

Hello My Names Are/Are Not

One of the strategies created by Vivian to help her students begin to unpack the positions from which they speak is through the use of the 'Hello my name is…" name tags that are widely used in settings both in and outside of school. In a re-design of this social naming tool, she has participants create a "Hello My Names Are" badge instead. This activity creates space for taking up the notion that we do not have an identity but rather multiple identities.

Hello My Names Are…

By Vivian Vasquez

Paulo Freire noted that once named, the world reappears as a problem that requires a new naming (2000). Janks (2010) reminds us, the power to name one's world breaks the silence. This activity is one opportunity for you to play with notions regarding naming practices, specifically the names, which we choose for ourselves, and the names, which are given to us or imposed upon us. This gets at the politics of our own location and the position(s) from which we speak, act, do and so forth as well as the ways in which we have been positioned and in what ways. What are the social practices associated with particular names; what Blye Frank (2010) refers to as our raced, classed, and gendered social practices, and why do we need to be mindful of these everyday practices?

Material/Procedures

1. On an index card, at the top write "Hello My Names Are" and write/ draw different names by which you are known. (See Figure 3.3.)

Hello my names are...
VIVIAN
Clippodcast
LASQUEZ
Ban
Mommy
Partner/ Wife
Dr.
Teacher
Professor

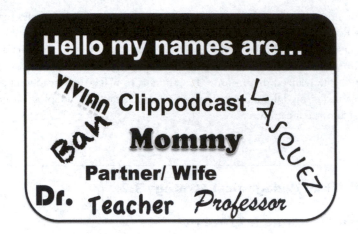

FIGURE 3.3 Hello my names are. . .

On a separate sheet of paper, write down each name/image and where it is used/recognized. How does each name position you and in what ways? What does each name mean in terms of access, privilege, disadvantage, and so forth. What are the positions from which you use each name? In which spaces do you use particular names, in what way, to achieve what ends, to do what sort(s) of life work? (See Figure 3.4.)

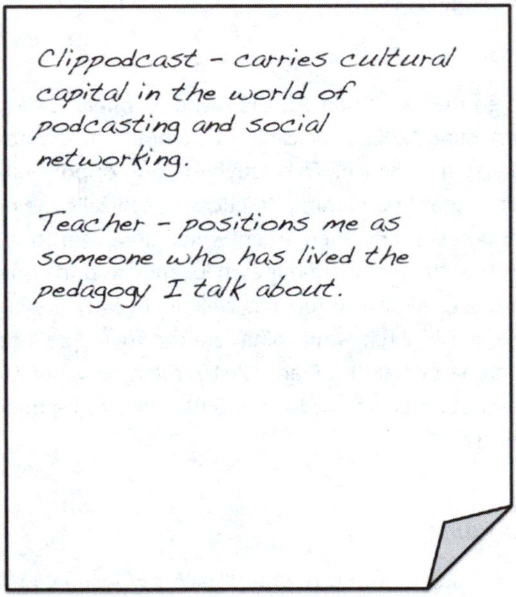

Clippodcast - carries cultural capital in the world of podcasting and social networking.
Teacher - positions me as someone who has lived the pedagogy I talk about.

FIGURE 3.4 Unpacking names.

2. On a second index card, at the top write "Hello My Names Are Not" then
    follow the same procedures as noted previously in #1. (See Figure 3.5.)

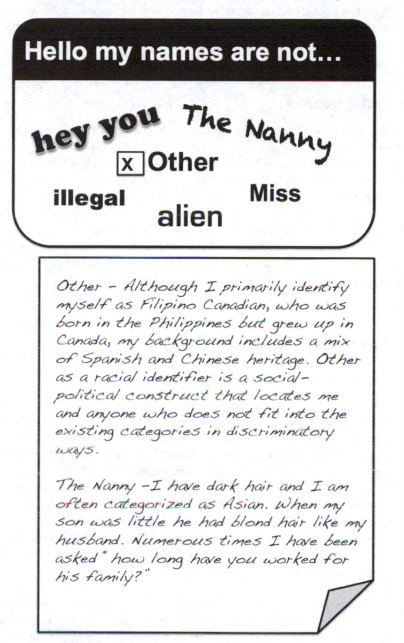

Hello my names are not...

hey you The Nanny

[X] Other

illegal   Miss

alien

Other – Although I primarily identify myself as Filipino Canadian, who was born in the Philippines but grew up in Canada, my background includes a mix of Spanish and Chinese heritage. Other as a racial identifier is a social-political construct that locates me and anyone who does not fit into the existing categories in discriminatory ways.

The Nanny – I have dark hair and I am often categorized as Asian. When my son was little he had blond hair like my husband. Numerous times I have been asked "how long have you worked for his family?"

FIGURE 3.5 Hello my names are not. . .

Have participants share their name cards in small groups and then with the large group and have them discuss the socio-political aspects of naming, including the notion that names help shape who we can and can't be as well as what we can and can't do. End with a discussion on how this impacts their ideological beliefs about teaching and learning.

Knowing Ourselves

Cruz's educational philosophy speaks to the notion that what we teach is who we are. He also provides a concrete example of philosophy development and what it takes to have it manifest in every aspect of teaching. Cruz's educational philosophy was not just sayings on paper, but was actualized in his theoretical and pedagogical understanding and his everyday living. In terms of theoretical knowledge, Cruz had an articulated belief about what he esteems about education. The theoretical knowledge that guides him is his understanding of philosopher Paulo Freire. While a teacher's practice is important, teachers are more likely to affect their students' lives when they have a deep understanding of why they do what they do.

TRY THIS: Pedagogical Strategy 3.3

Becoming Self-actualized: Historicizing the Self

This is an activity that has become one of the main assessments in one of Stacie's undergraduate courses. It is the result of listening to her students' needs and ways to support those needs. In this case the activity provides an opportunity for students to examine the role that personal stories, histories and legacies may play in shaping decision making in the classroom.

This activity may assist in constructing, analyzing and revising one's teaching philosophy from a critical literacy perspective. In the activity you are asked to consider multiple perspectives (i.e. your family's educational history) in order to understand the perspectives through which you speak and act. It is an opportunity to outgrow or build on your family history in order to form your own teaching philosophy.

1. Write about your family's educational history keeping in mind that "family" is broadly defined. Not everyone grows up in what society considers the "conventional family" (mother, father and siblings). Many people are raised by grandparents, adoptive parents, extended families, and institutions. In addition, many people have experienced

trauma within their families, which also shapes who they are and how they identify themselves. You may choose to write or not write about these traumatic experiences.

2.   How does history, privilege and power impact your family and their educational history/histories? Remember that this activity is designed to assist you in understanding how history and education have impacted you and your family, personally, but you do not need to share anything that makes you uncomfortable.

3.   Do you feel that you have been disadvantaged or marginalized in life in some way? What was the context of this disadvantage or marginalization? How might such experiences have impacted the way you participate in family, community, school and other places and contexts?

Maria Botelho adapted this personal history narrative exercise at the University of Massachusetts-Amherst. She believed that history is a written representation of the self that is open to interpretation. History may be told from many perspectives and through many voices, thus multiple histories exist within a society. As Loewen (1996) demonstrates in *Lies My Teacher Told Me*, some histories may "lie through omission" while others blatantly misrepresent facts. Histories are an ongoing series of social constructions, each representing the past at the particular present moment for particular present purposes.

Cruz's practice was not just developed through what he does in the classroom, but because he has a clear understanding of the theoretical perspective from which he engages in his teaching practice. In terms of his pedagogical knowledge, Cruz was able to state what he believed about education and enact it in his classroom. His classroom responsibilities chart was a demonstration of how his theoretical knowledge of Paulo Freire informed his practice. As a self-actualized teacher Cruz unpacked his ideological positions. He realized in order to be an effective teacher, part of his responsibility was to "reflect every day through theory about his practice" and to "make critical adjustments." Below are other recommendations to consider on a journey to "self-actualization" and becoming critically literate:

- *Self-reflexivity.* Teachers and researchers consider how theoretical and political assumptions, and beliefs become a part of the work that we do. While many researchers and teachers argue for objectivity and detachment, there is a need for an examination of who we are in order to "reveal what a researcher was positioned to see, to know and to understand" (Chiseri-Strater, 1996, p. 23).
- *Theoretical knowledge.* Remember Cruz had an articulated belief about what he esteems about education. The theoretical knowledge that guides Cruz is his understanding of philosopher Paulo Freire. While a teacher's practice is important, nothing can happen unless a teacher understands why they do

what they do. Cruz's practice is not just actualized by what he does in the classroom, but happens because he was able to talk about his practice through a theoretical lens.

- *Examining the personal in order to outgrow our current selves.* In unpacking our personal histories we begin to examine how what we believe may affect the decisions that we make. Examining our personal beliefs pushes us to seek understanding about our decisions and choices. This examination may push a new agenda that requires those of us who make the important decisions about education to examine and articulate how our personal philosophies or beliefs affect our decision making. This may allow you to re-think your position when you know that what you believe may not be as objective as you think.

Through philosophy development and self-examination, teachers can begin to outgrow their current practices, their current selves and beliefs in order to become better educators. As teachers we pride ourselves in knowing our students, but what we lack, is knowing ourselves, the position(s) from which we speak including both our strengths, and our weaknesses. Knowing that there are some teachers who would resist engaging in ways suggested in this chapter and book led us to include a variety of strategies and resources. We hope he have provided you with enough strategies and resources to support the needs of diverse teachers with whom you work. Having discussed ways to come to know ourselves, in the next three chapters, we turn to ways of using what we know about our students' interests to build a critical curriculum.

4

BUILDING CURRICULUM USING STUDENTS' INTERESTS

At the time that the Party Animals, discussed in Chapter 1, were brought to campus, Vivian and her colleague Sarah were exploring ways of creating spaces for critical literacies in the courses they were teaching. Vivian was teaching Literacy Courses and Sarah was teaching Social Studies Methods. Both of these were required courses for the pre-service teacher education program at their university. They used their students' interest in the Party Animals as an opportunity to build curriculum from a critical literacy perspective. In this chapter we will further unpack what happened as they created spaces in Vivian's literacy methods class to read the sculptures from a critical literacy perspective. She wanted her students to engage in critical readings as a way to make visible the complexities, patterns, trends, particularities, generalities, and/or discrepancies, in the information conveyed on the sculptures. Vivian knew some of the sculptures would be around for some time and they wanted their students to become critical consumers of this history in the making. As Luke and Freebody remind us (1997), how to teach literacy has to involve a moral, political, and cultural decision about the kind of literate practices needed to enhance both people's agency over their life trajectories or pathways and communities' intellectual, cultural and semiotic meaning-making resources.

Teaching Literacy that Takes Power Seriously

I refer to the approach to teaching literacy that takes power seriously as critical literacy.

(Janks, 2010, p. xiv)

We agree with Janks' perspective on critical literacy as we noted in Chapter 2 because it makes clear what difference it makes to frame literacy work in a critical way. Taking power seriously looks and sounds different in different set-tings. Whereas in one classroom you might find a group of children working to change an inequitable school practice (Vasquez, 2004;Vasquez & Felderman, 2013; Comber & Simpson, 2001), in another you might find a group of children work-ing in the community to disrupt injustice (Vasquez & Felderman, 2013; Comber & Nixon, 2008). There are some constants however, as noted by Janks in describ-ing a critical literacy teacher:

> A critical literacy teacher is … interested in what all kinds of texts (written, visual, and oral) do to readers, viewers, and listeners, and whose interests are served by what these texts do. They also help students to rewrite themselves and their local situations by helping them to pose problems and to act, often in small ways, to make the world a fairer place. Different orientations to working with critical literacy help them to do so.
>
> *(Janks, 2010, p. 19)*

Important to note is Janks' comment that critical literacy teachers help students to pose problems and to act because it is the action piece that is often missing from the university classroom. More than often students are asked to read, write, and discuss about critical literacy with the primary intent of helping students grow a knowledge base. Missing are opportunities for going out into the world and shift-ing the balance of power or changing inequitable situations or as Janks (2010) notes making the world a fairer place. This chapter and the next three chapters all offer demonstrations of possibility for engaging in critical literacies with adult learners that involve problem posing and/or engaging in some form of social action.

Under the umbrella of critical literacy as concerned with issues of language and power are key tenets with which we do literacy work. Those key tenets are as follows.

- Critical literacy involves having a critical perspective (Vasquez 2004; 1994).
- Students' cultural and multi-modal literacies should be respected and utilized in the university classroom.
- The world is a socially constructed text that can be read (Frank, 2008) and that when we read the word we simultaneously read the world (Freire & Macedo, 1987).
- All texts are socially constructed. That is texts are created by someone from a particular standpoint, position, point of view, or stance.
- Texts work to create particular subject positions meaning that texts are not only socially constructed, they are also socially constructive offering particular ways of being, doing, talking, and thinking that shift from context to context.
- Just as no text is neutral, natural, or normal, our reading of a text is never neutral, natural, or normal, either. Our readings of text are rooted in our discursive practices and the cultural models through which we live our lives.

- We can never speak outside of Discourse. As we engage with text or other people, we bring with us ways of being, doing, and thinking that help shape what we say and do.
- Critical literacy involves understanding the socio-political systems in which we live.
- Critical literacy practices can contribute to change (Freire & Macedo, 1987; Freebody & Luke, 1990; Vasquez, 2004).
- Text design and production can provide opportunities for critique and transformation (Larson and Marsh, 2005; Vasquez, 2005; Janks, 1993).

Researching the Everyday: Engaging in Systematic Observation

The photos in Figure 4.1 were taken by Vivian when the party animals were on display in Washington DC and on campus at the university where Vivian teaches.

(a)

(b)

FIGURE 4.1 (a) Yankee Doodle Donkey—Party Animal sculpture in Washington DC; (b) Party Animal elephant in Washington DC.

The animals were painted and adorned by local artists selected by the District of Columbia Commission on the Arts and Humanities. The artists were either individuals or groups—with about half of the artists residing in the District. The designs that they used, were selected by the Commission, from seven hundred proposals that came from around the world. Each artist was given a $1,000 grant and $200 for supplies to create the sculptures. According to a publicist for the project, corporations who chose to sponsor a donkey, elephant or both, provided funds and in-kind contributions toward the project.

As previously mentioned, for the most part as people in the community and tourists consumed these art pieces, they referred to the animals as fun, imaginative and whimsical. On the contrary, as depicted across the landscape in political cartoons and other print and media ads, for some time now "the menagerie of American political symbols have been reduced to what has become the dominant Democratic donkey and Republican elephant" (Sullivan, 1996, n.p., para. 2).

Take the history of the democratic donkey, for instance. When Andrew Jackson ran for president in 1828, his opponents tried to label him a "jackass" for his populist views and his slogan, "Let the people rule." Political cartoonist Thomas Nast became frustrated with Republicans in the 1870s, when he felt the party had strayed from social liberalism. That frustration, in part, spawned the Republican elephant image as bungling, stupid, pompous and conservative. As longstanding political symbols there is really nothing whimsical or imaginative about the choice of donkeys and elephants. In fact the use of elephants and donkeys served to punctuate the dominance of two political parties over all the others. In some ways this dominance has been normalized and yet there is nothing normal or natural about that.

REFLECTION POINT 4.1

- Make a list of the political parties in the country where you reside. How many did you name? Was creating this list easy or challenging?
- Do a Google search to find out about the various political parties in your country beyond those on your list.
- What surprised you?

Pedagogical Strategy 4.1 focuses on one way to disrupt normalized ways of being. Using the strategy students are asked to locate and name various symbols found in their everyday lives. They are then asked to unpack and critically analyze the symbols by exploring its historical significance as well as the effects of such symbols on its consumers. Included in the pedagogy box are discussion questions to further engage with the ideas previously mentioned.

TRY THIS: Pedagogical Strategy 4.1

Unpacking the Everyday

Use the following chart in Figure 4.2 with your students to unpack symbols found in the everyday world that have taken on normalized status.

Symbol from the everyday world. e.g. sports team mascot	Place where symbol is found	Historical significance of the symbol	Real world effects on consumers of the symbol

FIGURE 4.2 Unpacking the Party Animals.

In the first column, have them list symbols they encounter in their everyday lives such as symbols used to represent sports team mascots or symbols used to represent department stores. In column two they are to list the place(s) where these symbols are located. In the third column have them note the historical significance of each symbol. Finally, in the fourth column have them jot down the effects of each of the symbols on those who consume them or read them in their everyday life.

Discuss the following:

1. What difference do these symbols make? For whom? In what ways?
2. How can such dominance be disrupted or problematized?
3. What sorts of social action can be taken to effect change?

Critically Reading the Party Animals

In order to help their students read the party animals from a critical literacy perspective, Vivian and Sarah created a viewing guide (see Figure 4.3), which consisted of a chart in which students were asked to make observations regarding the various text and images that were painted on each figure. Using the chart, students were asked to look closely at how language is used on the sculptures including: How are headlines, words, and phrases used? By whom? For what purpose(s)? They also looked closely at socio-cultural representations on the sculptures including: who is represented and who is not represented based on race, class, ethnicity, age, religion, and gender.

While doing this critical observation work, their students engaged in socio-political readings of the Party Animals, which led them to consider the subject positions (ways of being, doing, thinking) for different individuals and groups

Critically Reading the Party Animals

Donkeys	'Reading' Prompts	Elephants
	Socio-cultural Representations **Who is represented? Who is not?** race, class, ethnicity, age, religion, gender	
	Grammar of Visual Images How are symbols, images, local/global scenes and everyday artifacts incorporated and used in the design of the Party Animals?	
	Language Use •How are headlines, words, and phrases used? By whom? For what purpose(s)? •How are pronouns used? •How is humor used?	
	Ideological References •What/whose values and beliefs are promoted? In what ways? •Whose values and beliefs are not promoted? •Who is privileged/marginalized by these ideological references? •Where/how is power located? •Who sponsored the animal? •What are the institutional connections?	

FIGURE 4.3   Party Animals viewing guide.

of people, conveyed by the images and text on the various animals. For instance some students focused on gender issues and the objectification of women in such sculptures as the donkey in Figure 4.4. This particular animal has large exaggerated lips painted bright red. The hind legs are adorned in what appears to resemble fish net stockings. The combination of bright red lips and the fish net stockings are symbols often associated with promiscuity. This animal is also adorned with several pieces of jewelry including a strand of white pearls and large white fashion glasses. Many of the donkey's adornments are exaggerated making it look both vampy and laughable. The problematic representation of women is even more obvious when compared to some of the male donkeys such as the Yankee Doodle Donkey in Figure 4.1a. Whereas the male donkey is completely clothed with top hat and tie, the female donkey is given a dress with a plunging neckline to expose cleavage. The back of the female donkey is also exposed due to its open back dress.

Other students also explored what they felt was missing from the texts. For instance they took stock of the various ethnicities and cultures represented on the animals. This proved to be challenging, as they had to seek out the various animals in other places around the District. While engaging in this exploration

FIGURE 4.4 Female donkey.

however, they did discover that those things that did appear on the animals had gone through approval at some point in the process. For instance they learned that the People for the Ethical Treatment of Animals group (PETA) had submitted an entry to decorate one of the elephants. Apparently the arts commission believed animal cruelty was an inappropriate topic to present to the public. PETA's design was of a teary-eyed elephant with its right front leg chained in shackles. According to a *Washington Post* report (Tucker, 2002) Anthony Gittens, executive director of the arts commission, had denounced the design noting the party animal was being used as a political billboard. At PETA's appeal, in a 27 page opinion document, U.S. District Judge Richard J. Leon ruled that PETA's design was wrongly denied by the D.C. Commission on the Arts and Humanities given that they had allowed other groups to display donkey and elephant icons with subtle or overt messages (Tucker, 2002). PETA's offering for the street art project is shown in Figure 4.5. The elephant wears a blanket with the following words printed on it: "THE CIRCUS IS COMING, SEE SHACKLES—BULL HOOKS—LONELINESS ALL UNDER THE 'BIG TOP'. "

This exploration was a wonderful experience in understanding how texts are socially constructed, by whom and for what purpose. It was also a very good experience in seeing how language and images work in powerful ways toward positioning readers in particular ways. This exploration also made clear to Vivian and Sarah's students how the process of the social construction of text can be politically charged as in the censorship of the PETA design.

FIGURE 4.5 PETA Party Animal.

Re-thinking the Syllabus

Interest in reading the sculptures on campus led to students analyzing even those sculptures that were not located on campus but in other parts of the city. This led to further critical readings of art pieces and monuments. Given this interest Vivian decided to alter one of the course assignments turning it into a personal inquiry whereby students who were interested could propose to do a research project based on critically reading everyday texts, public art or monuments. For these students she recommended reading Loewen's (1999) *Lies Across America: What Our Historic Sites Get Wrong* and Loewen's (1996) *Lies My Teacher Told Me: Everything Your American History Textbook Got Wrong.*

Using Loewen's books as a framework for critically analyzing monuments, a group of students looked closely at various monuments in Washington DC with an eye for the texts and images included in the monuments and how such texts and images position the visitor/viewer/reader in particular ways. One of the monuments that particularly piqued their interest was the Jefferson Memorial located by the Tidal Basin in Washington DC. In Loewen's book *Lies Across American*, he refers to a quote inscribed on one of the walls of the memorial that had been altered because the original text simply did not fit. The altered text reads: "… We … solemnly publish and declare, that these Colonies are and of right ought to be free and independent states …" (Loewen, 1999). According to Loewen (1999) omitting "United" before "Colonies" results in the insinuation that the thirteen separate states declared independence. There were several other such alterations and omissions at this particular monument alone. In his book Loewen identifies numerous such "lies" in monuments across the United States.

To make their findings accessible to others Vivian's students created a Zine, which is a small self-published book that they distributed to visitors at various locations in Washington DC.

TRY THIS: Pedagogical Strategy 4.2

Martin Luther King Memorial

In spite of such books as *Lies Across America* (Loewen, 1999), omissions and inconsistencies continue to plague monuments and public art. More recently controversy arose over some text inscribed on the newly erected Martin Luther King Memorial in Washington DC. Ironically this monument is not too far away from the Jefferson Memorial.

- Have a look at Figure 4.6—a photo of the memorial with the quote in question. The quote reads, "I was a drum major for justice, peace and righteousness."

- Search the Internet or YouTube for a clip of the actual speech given by Martin Luther King from which the quote was taken.
- What is the difference between what Dr. King said in his speech versus what was placed on the monument?
- What differences made a difference?
- How is the meaning changed from the actual speech to the monument?
- How does the monument position you as a viewer?

FIGURE 4.6   Martin Luther King Memorial.

Inquiry into Space and Place

As the class engaged in a socio-political reading of the sculptures as a whole they wondered whether the party animals that were brought to campus were being shielded form potential damage by protestors who were in town, at the time, for the 2002 Annual Meetings of the International Monetary Fund and the World Bank Group which were being held in Washington DC. Since the donkeys and elephants were earmarked for auction, to the highest bidders, Vivian's students' theorized that it was possible and very likely that the sculptures were brought to campus to keep them in good shape in order to fetch top dollar.

REFLECTION POINT 4.2

Before reading further say something about Vivian's students' socio-political reading and theorizing regarding the placement of the Party Animals.

Two of Vivian's students called the *DC Commission* on the *Arts* and Humanities to confirm their suspicions. Their calls were either not returned or their questions not answered. A few days later one of the students discovered a report released by PR Newswire United Business Media stating the following:

> The first 69 sculptures were removed from the downtown area of Washington DC in the Foggy Bottom, Farragut West, Farragut North, McPherson Square, Metro Center and Federal Triangle neighborhoods. These locations were chosen due to safety concerns for the Party Animals during the International Monetary Fund and World Bank meetings from September 25–29.
>
> *(http://www.prnewswire.com/news-releases/party-animals-removed-from-streets-to-protect-them-from-imf-demonstrators-75904192.html; PR Newswire United Business Media)*

Although the report acknowledged that the sculptures had been brought to campus due to safety concerns it did not address whose safety was in question and why such safety was a concern. Was it the safety of the protestors that worried officials in the District? Or were Vivian's students correct in assuming that it was the sculptures that were being shielded from the protestors? If so, were city officials assuming the protest would result in the defacement or destruction of such things as the party animals? A damaged sculpture could result in lower bids for purchase at the auction to be held later in the year. This clearly was problematic for the folks at the DC Arts Commission who had already earmarked possible funds raised for use in grant programs for the arts and arts education in Washington DC.

This experience worked to help the students to have more of a discerning eye, a healthy skepticism as noted by Luke (2007) in the Ontario Numeracy and Literacy Secretariat video on critical literacy. Nevertheless, they found great pleasure and excitement in doing this kind of work. This in fact is exactly what Vivian (Vasquez, 2005) found in her study on Negotiating Critical Literacies with Young Children; critical literacies when built from the interests of children are both powerful and pleasurable.

This critical reading generated other critical readings of the art pieces. For instance one of Vivian student's began to explore where each of the Party Animals were placed. She discovered that a majority of the sculptures were located in Northwest DC where most of the tourist attractions, affluent neighborhoods, and embassies are located. She noticed very few were located in Southeast DC, the southeastern quadrant of Washington DC, where there is a high population of African Americans and which has the unfair reputation of being a disadvantaged, high crime area in spite of the fact that there are middle class neighborhoods in SE. This student went as far as to contact the Commission with regards to who made the decision regarding where to place the animals. Her attempts were met with resistance. Frustrated, and determined to take action in some way, she wrote a paper about this situation and presented it at a national conference for literacy teachers and researchers.

Another student problematized the fact that one of the sculptures had been placed on top of chalk art created by students from the university. The chalk art was promoting an event organized by other students. Vivian's students discussed whose art counts and who decides whose art counts. They argued that the chalk work done by the other students was also art that should have been respected and that the sculpture that rested on top of it could have been placed in a number of other places at the university.

Another student became interested in finding out which organizations sponsored elephants and which organizations sponsored donkeys given the symbolic use of these animals to represent the two dominant political parties.

TRY THIS: Pedagogical Strategy 4.3

Adapting Critical Readings

- Adapt the reading prompts used to read the Party Animals as they appear in Figure 4.3.
- How might you use a version of this chart in your setting to help the adults you are working with to read such things as monuments, public art and landmarks from a critical literacy perspective?

Vivian and Sarah, in their work with the Party Animals attempted to avoid simply talking the talk but having their students live rather than read or hear about a critical literacy curriculum. Even more importantly rather than delivering a purely paper-based curriculum, they negotiated the curriculum in the same way.

In the next chapter we continue to explore possibilities for critical literacies in the university classroom with a focus on challenging commonplace thinking.

5

CHALLENGING COMMONPLACE THINKING

Curriculum is a metaphor for the lives you want everyone to live and the people you want everyone to be. A critical literacy curriculum has many goals, two of which are disrupting the commonplace and interrogating multiple perspectives. While it is important to talk about each of these goals, it is best to do so based on pre-service and in-service teachers having experienced each of these goals firsthand. This is what we mean by living the curriculum.

In this chapter and the next are examples of how we have organized our pre-service and in-service sessions to challenge commonplace thinking and to explore multiple perspectives. In this chapter we will show how we have addressed disrupting the commonplace using adolescent and children's literature and everyday text. In the next chapter we will focus on using a combination of children's literature and art to explore multiple perspectives.

We highlight adolescent and children's literature in our pre-service and in-service classes for a number of reasons. First, the use of literature in a pre-service and in-service teacher education program is an historical expectation, which teachers can use to expand and support a more inclusive and critical notion of literacy. Based on our shared experience in teacher education, we can confidently say that in every literacy course we have taught there are always at least two or more students who begin to talk about children's books or adolescent novels before we do and so our experience is that, the use of such texts is an inter-est for teacher education students. Second, one of the trends in adolescent and children's literature is the publication of what we describe as "social issue texts," or literature that addresses the socio-political issues that students may face on a day-to-day basis. Together, we argue, these reasons make adolescent and children's literature one way to create spaces for much needed critical conversations in teacher education.

Exploring Systems of Meaning

To illustrate the importance of disrupting the commonplace, one of the books that we use is *I'm Glad I'm a Boy! I'm Glad I'm a Girl!* (Darrow, 1970). An excerpt from the text begins with objects boys and girls own, "Boys have trucks/Girls have dolls," followed by activities in which boys and girls participate, "Boys are Cub Scouts/Girls are Brownies," which then leads to differences in behaviors, "Boys are strong/Girls are graceful" (pp. 1–6). The book then ultimately identifies specific jobs that boys and girls take on, "Boys are doctors/Girls are nurses" (pp. 9–10); "Boys are pilots/Girls are stewardesses"; "Boys are presidents/Girls are first ladies" (pp. 15–18).

We start with this out-of-print book written in the 1970s (accessed online at http://www.funlobby.com/index.php/200905051186/im-glad-im-a-boy-im-glad-im-a-girl.html) to demonstrate how to help students identify and define various "systems of meaning" operating upon or within texts. We tell teachers that the term, "systems of meaning" is somewhat difficult to define. In reality "systems of meaning" are assumptions (often stereotypes) being made about how the world operates. Systems of meaning are rarely stated, but rather, are societal forces at play which show up in the language that is used and how this language positions the reader. One of the systems of meaning operating in *I'm Glad I'm a Boy! I'm Glad I'm a Girl* is the notion that boys and girls play and embody particular roles. Without saying anything more, we ask students to turn to a partner and identify other systems of meaning that are operating and, together with their partner, generate a definition for the term "systems of meaning."

Although a sexist perspective is blatant in this book, pre-service and in-service teachers often forgive the authors because the book was written some thirty years ago. "Things are different now," they say. Rather than argue this point, we invite students to do a bit of inquiry by asking them to look through a range of texts we have collected—other picture books, newspapers, magazines, posters—and look for assumptions being made. After providing pre-service and in-service teachers some time to browse these texts we ask them to share one thing they found. Without fail, students find that stereotypical assumptions abound. While they may not be as blatant as those in *I'm Glad I'm a Boy! I'm Glad I'm a Girl*, they are just as insidious (sex still sells, smart people are still portrayed as nerds, bullies are still boys, fat people are still jolly). We end this discussion by writing "No text is neutral" on whatever surface we have available (blackboard, white board, flip chart) and ask participants what saying this—"No text is neutral"—means relative to literacy learning and instruction.

REFLECTION POINT 5.1

No Text is Neutral

- What comes to mind when you see the phrase "No text is neutral"?
- What kinds of texts do you think this refers to?
- Have you ever talked about texts in this way? If yes—why? If no—why not?

Disrupting the Commonplace as a Disposition

While one experience at disrupting the commonplace begins to create awareness, it is hardly enough to insure that it has become a disposition. Disrupting the commonplace is not easy or natural. What it requires is for us to become aware of the assumptions we have in the past just taken for granted. In a sense it is like asking humans to become aware of the air they breathe. Doing it once might be fine, but being aware of every breath is asking a lot.

Let us be clear about what we believe about literacy teaching and learning. While we believe in quality language encounters, rather than quantity language encounters, it is important that pre-service and in-service teachers experience ongoing opportunities to unpack the systems of meaning that are operating in and upon the texts they encounter in daily life. To this end, we often begin each session by reading a children's book (for a list of books that raise important social issues refer to Resource Box 5.1) and by asking students questions such as:

- What issues or stereotypes do you see being addressed?
- What do you find problematic?
- How does this text position you as a reader?
- Who is advantaged or disadvantaged?
- Who is missing from the storyline?
- From what perspective(s) are you reading the text?

RESOURCE BOX 5.1

Books that Focus on Social Issues

Anderson, M.T. (2012). *Feed.* Sommerville, MA: Candlewick Press.
An adolescent novel, set in the future that focuses on issues of identity and positioning, power, control, and consumerism, in a society where people connect to the Internet via feeds implanted in their brains.

Boston Weatherford, C. (2007). *Freedom on the menu.* New York, NY: Puffin Books.
This story is set in Greensboro, North Carolina, in 1960 and focuses on a story of desegregation from the viewpoint of a young girl.

Bruchac, J. (2004). *Hidden roots.* New York, NY: Scholastic.
This is the story of Sonny who comes to learn that he is Abenaki. Written by a Native author, the book focuses on why his Native heritage has been kept secret. As the secret unfolds we learn of the Vermont Eugenics Project, a shameful government sterilization program that ended in 1936. The story creates space for learning about this brutal policy inflicted on American Indians.

Campbell, N.I. & LaFave, K. (2005). *Shi-shi-etko.* Toronto, ON: Groundwood Press.
Written by Native authors this book focuses on the experiences of a brother and sister who are forced to attend residential schools, the Canadian equivalent of US boarding schools for Native children due to government policy. Issues of Native identity, the richness of Native life, positioning, disadvantage, power and control are reflected.

Mickenberg, J.L. (2010). *Tales for little rebels: A collection of radical children's literature.* New York, NY: NYUPress.
A collection of over forty stories, poems, comic strips, primers, and other texts for children that reflect issues like peace, gender equality, environmental responsibility, and civil rights.

Tan , S. (2007) *The arrival.* New York, NY: Arthur A. Levine Books.
Focuses on the immigrant experience creating space for conversations about displacement, domination, access, diversity, privilege, disadvantage, and positioning.

We allocate the first half hour of each class session to this activity. Resource Box 5.2 lists some of the children's books that we used in a recent study that we conducted (Albers, Harste & Vasquez, 2011). We initially went through and identified all of the underlying assumptions that we thought were being made in each text. In *Willy & Hugh* (Browne, 2000) we identified 21 issues or stereotypes being perpetuated including "Nerds are little," "Bullies are big," "Bullies disrupt belonging which causes marginalization," "Nerds are weak, wimpy," "Bullies are mean, tough," "Unlikely characters can have meaningful relationships," "Courage is not related to size," "Little people need big people to protect them,"

"Don't judge people by their physical size," and so on. Resource Box 5.2 lists, for the three books used in this study, the issues and stereotypes most frequently identified by participants as well as those most infrequently identified. Over time participants did begin to identify more and more assumptions. For the most part, however, they identified, on the average, five assumptions. Even the teacher who consistently identified the greatest number of stereotypes only identified seven (regardless of the number that were actually present in the book). For us, this further demonstrated the need for us to continue to create spaces to find ways to support teachers in having these important critical conversations.

REFLECTION POINT 5.2

Self as Informant

- When you were a young learner what kinds of experiences did you have in school with regards to unpacking underlying assumptions in books or critically analyzing books?
- How might previous experiences with critically analyzing text impact one's ability to identify underlying social issues and assumptions embedded in those texts?

RESOURCE BOX 5.2

Children's Books Used to Disrupt the Commonplace

Book	Most Frequent Issues and Stereotypes Identified	Least Frequent Issues and Stereotypes Identified
Willy & Hugh (Browne, 2000)	• Nerds are little. • Bullies are big. • Bullies disrupt belonging which causes marginalization. • Nerds are weak, wimpy. • Bullies are mean, tough. • Unlikely characters can have meaningful relationships.	• One needs friends to be happy. • Names reflect personalities. • Nerds wear sweater vests and chinos. • Don't judge people by their physical appearance.

Book	Most Frequent Issues and Stereotypes Identified	Least Frequent Issues and Stereotypes Identified
Sister Anne's Hands (Lorbiecki, 1998)	• Being a minority member in a dominant culture causes problems. • Teachers should be of the same ethnicity as the students they teach. • Powerful institutions, like churches, have a particular social responsibility to wash their dirty laundry in public rather than sweep it under the rug. • Parents have a right to pull their children out of class if they are unhappy with the quality of teaching. • Nuns are representatives of a church that teaches tolerance, equality and acceptance.	• Larger social forces influence childhood beliefs and attitudes. • Parents should be careful about what they say in front of children. • Forgive wrong-doing: Do unto others as you would have them do unto you. • The unknown is something to be avoided.
Into the Forest (Browne, 2004)	• Intact families give children security while single-parent families, absent father families, or broken families are associated with fear, anxiety, and insecurity. • Fairy tales often play with the notion of children left to their own devices and often have characters that act like wolves. • Adults reinforce fears by not offering explanations. • Forests are dark and scary where bad things happen. • Girls need protection while boys can be left on their own.	• Boys ignore rules. • Women (girls) are nurturers while men (boys) are not. • Old women (grandmothers) are both weak and fragile. • Children are lost and rather helpless without an adult around. • Authors use stormy weather to signal that something is amiss.

Extending and Expanding What "Disrupting the Commonplace" Entails

One device we have used to extend and expand pre-service and in-service teachers' notions of disrupting the commonplace are curriculum invitations. In our workshops and classes we often focus an entire session to exploring curriculum invitations. Curricular invitations are activity-like centers to which students go in partnership or small groups. Invitations are opportunities for participants to take a new perspective or try a new approach to a topic or issue they already have some sense about. Following is an example of an invitation.

TRY THIS: Pedagogical Strategy 5.1

Becoming a Text Analyst

This invitation builds on the work of Luke and Freebody (1997). Included is a set of directions inviting participants to use the questions which Luke and Freebody recommend as tools for examining the materials (a children's book, a book club order form, a teen magazine, and a community flyer of some sort) we have put at the center.

- Who wrote this text?
- For what purpose?
- How would it be different if someone different had written this text?
- How do these authors position their readers?
- How might the text be constructed differently?
- What past experiences are informing your reading of this text?

Participants are usually asked to work with a partner with whom they can discuss responses to the questions. At the end of the "Invitations Workshop" participants share a surprise they learned at any of the curriculum invitations they tried. "Becoming a Text Analyst" can be kept fresh by changing the materials that participants are asked to analyze. To support the taking ownership of this invitation, participants can be invited to bring in texts that they encounter in their daily lives, which they believe merit interrogation.

TRY THIS: Pedagogical Strategy 5.2

Disrupting the Commonplace: Curricular Invitations

Following is a list of other curricular invitations that support participants in disrupting the commonplace assumptions underlying texts.

1. Chart-a-Conversation

Provide groups of three students with a one-page sheet with four columns headings: Things We Like; Things We Dislike; Patterns We See; Issues and Stereotypes. Have them read a children's book (you might start out with something as simple as *Where the Wild Things Are*, Sendak, 1963) and ask them to discuss the book in terms of each of these categories writing down their decisions on the worksheet. Have them share and compare their conclusions with other groups. The issues and stereotypes category often begins critical conversations. In the case of *Where the Wild Things Are* issues arise over whether or not parents should use food as a punishment, why books that have been around such a long time are getting more expensive rather than cheaper, why some parent groups have banned the book because they see it as encouraging imaginative thinking and talking back to parents.

(Originally developed by Pat Smith, Bathurst, Australia.)

2. One Connection, One Observation, One Question, One Surprise

Ask participants to read a children's book of your choice. Ask each person at the center to record (and afterwards) share one connection, one observation, one question and one surprise they found by reading the book. As a culminating experience ask participants in explore: (1) the assumptions behind the question each participant asked, and (2) how they might answer the questions that each participant in the group generated.

(Originally developed by Jennifer Story, Honolulu, Hawaii.)

3. Quotable Quotes

Provide participants at this center with a stack of 3 × 5 cards and a short thought-provoking professional article to read (for ideas see the Thought Pieces in Lewison, Leland, & Harste, 2008). Have students record a quote they found insightful on side one of their 3 × 5 card and what they want to say about it on side two of their card. Have them collect and shuffle the 3 × 5 cards, share them one by one as a group, and discuss what they personally made of the quote prior to the author having the last word by reading what they wrote on the back side of their 3 × 5 card. As a group students might explore what assumptions were being made by the author that called his or her attention to this particular quote.

(Originally developed by Carolyn Burke, Bloomington, Indiana.)

4. Target, Perpetrator, Ally, Bystander

Orally read your selection of children's book that raises an important social issue, and a worksheet with four columns which read, "Target," "Perpetrator," "Ally," and "Bystander." Have participants select one of the books to read aloud and then together identify who they see as the target, the perpetrator, the allies, and the bystanders in the book. Have participants leave their worksheet at the center so that after other groups have completed the engagement, they might look at how other groups have responded. Discuss why there are often different answers as to which characters played what roles.

(Originally developed by Linda Christensen, Portland, Oregon.)

Disrupting the Commonplace Through the Production of Counter-narratives

Researchers (Boler & Zembylas, 2003) have found that students learn more about what it means to take on a critical stance by actually re-designing texts than they do by critiquing texts that already exist. Counter-narratives are texts that are created to talk back to the original problematic text. One of the curricular engagements we have used to this end is the re-design of everyday advertisements. This activity stems from our students' interactions with everyday texts such as print ads in the world around them and posters often found on school bulletin boards or in school hallways. After experiencing some work with critical literacies such as through working with children's books and adolescent novels, students begin to notice socio-political issues in other kinds of texts including print advertisements and school posters. They often begin to make connections between the critical analysis work with children's books and these everyday texts.

Working with Print Ads

In one study that Vivian and Jerry conducted with Peggy Albers (Albers, Harste, & Vasquez, 2010) they invited pre-service and in-service teachers to redesign advertisements. We will focus on two such advertisements in this chapter. The first advertisement is a McDonald's ad featuring a Big Mac Burger with the phrase "Are you Mac enough?" The second is a Ralph Lauren ad featuring a young blonde girl wearing a light colored flowered, summer short-sleeve dress with a sweater over her shoulders and print across the top reading "Ralph Lauren Children."

Participants, working in groups of five or six, were given one half hour to create a counter-narrative poster using a variety of art materials we had provided. The results as shown in Figure 5.1 were quite stunning. What made this engagement

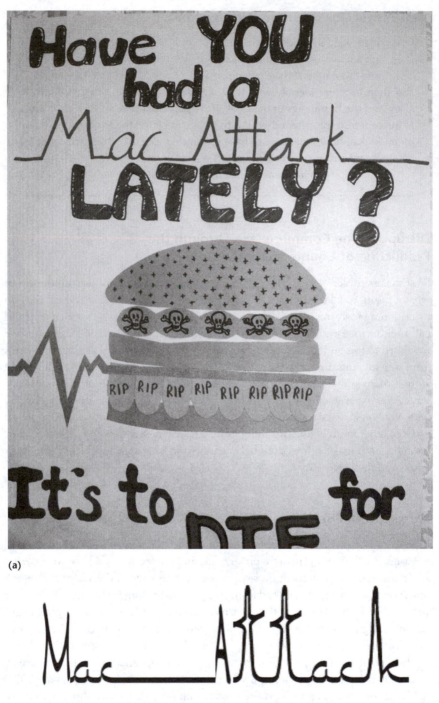

(a)

(b)

(c)

FIGURE 5.1 (a) Mac Attack poster; (b) Mac Attack electrocardiogram; (c) Counter ad poster.

so exciting was that participants first had to unpack the original advertisement, critique what was said, critique what wasn't being said, and then create a counter-narrative that spoke back to and disrupted the original text. They then were asked to talk about the perspective or positioning from which they crafted their counter-text. Knowing or naming the position from which one speaks is an important part of being able to speak from another position regardless of whether that is a counter position or complimentary position.

The group that created the counter ad in Figure 5.1a played with the late seventies advertising campaign for McDonald's that centered on the irresistibility of a Big Mac. Commercial after commercial showed people having a Big Mac Attack® as they longed for the hamburger. The ads often described these impending attacks as something that could happen just about anywhere—while you're working, watching TV, swimming or reading. The ads go on to say that at any point in time one could suddenly have an irresistible craving for a Big Mac sandwich—a Big Mac Attack®.

In the counter ad in Figure 5.1a, the actual words used in the ad campaign are co-opted and re-contextualized so that the ad ends up working against itself. In the McDonald's ad campaign, eating a Big Mac is the cure for the "attack". In contrast, in the counter ad, it is the Big Mac that kills. The words "Mac Attack" are written in such a way that the letters resemble the lines on an electrocardiogram tape as shown in Figure 5.1b.

This group of teachers also co-opted the slang term "It's to die for!" which was born in the 1970s to indicate great longing. The phrase has often been used by well known TV persona such as Samantha on the show *Sex and the City* when talking about clothing or food. It has also been used sarcastically to deceive as in the following exchange between Simba and Scar, two characters from *The Lion King* (1994). Simba is heir to the throne. His father is Mufasa. Mufasa and Scar are brothers. Throughout the movie Scar deviously finds ways to overthrow the throne in order to become King.

Scar:	Now you wait here. Your father has a marvelous surprise for you.
Simba:	Oooh. What is it?
Scar:	If I told you, it wouldn't be a surprise, now would it?
Simba:	If you tell me, I'll still act surprised.
Scar:	Ho ho ho. You are such a naughty boy!
Simba:	Come on, Uncle Scar.
Scar:	No, no, no, no, no, no, no. This is just for you and your daddy. You know, a sort of…father–son…thing. Well! I'd better go get him.

The exchange takes place as Scar attempts to lure Simba to his death. The conversation continues.

Simba:	Oh, okay. Hey, Uncle Scar, will I like this surprise?
Scar:	Simba, it's to die for!

These words have become such a widely used hyperbole that when Lake Superior State University (LSSU) released its annual Banished Words List for 1995, "It's to die for" was on the list. On their website (located at http://www.lssu.edu/banishcd/archive/1995.php), LSSU points out that "… people have a tendency to over-use and most often, mis-use words sometimes to the point where the words or phrases become generally useless." They go on to say phrases like "to die for … for instance have been beaten to a pulp" and that "these words started out as interesting and useful but alas, they eventually became as pleasant to the ears as the sound of fingernails scratching on a chalkboard."

In their counter ad, the group of teachers combined the use of the two popular phrases "Mac Attack" and "It's to die for" implying that eating foods like Big Macs could cause a heart attack and result in death. In the case of the unhealthiness of fast foods, this would be a slow death because fast foods have become so good at creating ad campaigns that easily become normalized that consumers often buy in without considering the effects of their decisions. The exaggerated nature of the counter ad is meant to stress the importance of being an informed consumer while simultaneously spoofing a well known ad campaign.

This work with teachers showed that having the opportunity to produce a counter ad in collaboration with others—so participants could talk through aspects of visual literacy—supported teachers in taking on a critical stance as well as thinking semiotically about sign systems and how they mean. Following is a pedagogical strategy to explore analyzing texts and counter-texts.

TRY THIS: Pedagogical Strategy 5.3

Analyzing Texts and Counter-texts

The second ad we introduced in this chapter is the Ralph Lauren ad featuring a young blonde girl wearing a light colored flowered, summer short-sleeve dress with a white sweater over her shoulders and the words "Ralph Lauren Children" behind the girl's head, close to the top of the page. The counter ad created for this ad is Figure 5.1c.

Frame your reading of the counter ad from the perspective of the original ad as described previously and discuss the following questions.

- What systems of meaning were the creators of the counter ad attempting to make visible or problematized?
- What might be the intent of including the various words and images?
- For whom might this ad be targeted?
- What would you need to know about the history of Rosedale to better understand the possible intent of the ad? Here is a website for the

Rosedale Real Estate For Sale site that may be useful in your analysis: http://www.rosedalerealestateforsale.com/

- How might understanding some of the history of the place (Rosedale) named on the counter ad help you to read the ad differently?
- Try your hand at creating your own counter ad for either the McDonald's ad or the Ralph Lauren ad. After doing so engage in an analysis of your own counter ad.

Disrupting the Commonplace: Some In-process Thoughts

Critical literacy asks pre-service and in-service teachers to teach literacy in a way that they have not in all likelihood experienced themselves. This is why disrupting the commonplace has to be an ongoing theme throughout one's work with these teachers and why we believe they need opportunities to live such experiences themselves.

Some key understandings follow:

1. Effective teachers of literacy need to understand—and in turn help students understand—that texts position readers to read in particular ways.
2. Literacy in the 21st-century classroom needs to make students aware as well as have tools to speak to and against these systems of meaning.
3. Multiple engagements with multiple texts provide multiple perspectives on complex issues and diminish the chance of being satisfied with simplistic solutions.
4. Critical literacy is not a spectator sport, but rather requires active engagement and inquiring minds. To read passively is to read a text uncritically. To see "comprehension" as the goal of our literacy program is no longer good enough. We need to create a critically literate citizenry, and critically literate citizens need to be able to unpack the underlying systems of meaning that operate in a text.

Allan Luke (2009) goes so far as to pose critical literacy as a basic human right. He notes that

> ... in today's environment if you don't have critical literacy you are a sucker, you are going to wind up in debt, you are going to end up on the streets, you are going to sign up with the first bank that offers you a crummy mortgage, you are going to wind up with a big Visa card debt, you are going to buy everything that is pushed your way.
>
> *(running count 2990 at video opening)*

"Texts," argues Janks (2010, p. xii) "have designs on you." In order to be critically literate, we, as consumers, must be able to read between and behind the lines. Peggy Albers (2007) says that by analyzing visual information and teaching students to do the same, we provide them with needed tools to interrogate the very lifestyles they are being sold and to question that bill of goods.

We wish to argue that by engaging in discussions of how texts position us, students become agents, rather than victims, of texts. In order to navigate through the plethora of texts that bombard us—print text, visual texts, audio texts, video texts, musical texts—citizens have to be able to have and to take agency. This involves understanding how texts are framed and how they position us as readers, how information is accessed, received, produced and internalized through multimodal means, and how to read critically and critique all types of texts. As educators, we must support students' abilities to take multiple perspectives, interrogate intent, reposition themselves in the world, and understand that despite any altruistic motives, we all have had and continue to have our hands in the cookie jar. There is no moral high ground to which any of us can scamper. No claiming we have arrived. There is only ongoing vigilance and a growing cognizance of the work that lies ahead both for ourselves, the teachers we teach, as well as the students that they reach. In the next chapter we explore what it means to interrogate and read the word and the world from multiple perspectives.

6
INTERROGATING MULTIPLE PERSPECTIVES

Imagining the World from the Perspective of Others

Interrogating multiple perspectives is done for purposes of imagining what the world looks like from the perspective of others or from other theoretical orientations. While we are continually involved in making judgments about what has occurred, who is powerful, what is right, and what is just, these assessments are usually made from our own perspective; our own take on the world; our own ideological beliefs. By making the interrogation of multiple perspectives a routine social practice in pre-service and in-service education, we are in fact demonstrating that we value multiple realities and identities, and that there are no single truths. We further demonstrate that diversity and difference is more important than conformity and consensus.

Similar to disrupting the commonplace, one way we explore multiple perspectives is by introducing a children's book and asking participants to respond in a variety of ways. One of our favorite books for this purpose is *Fox* (2006) by Margaret Wild. We describe how we use this text below in Pedagogical Strategy 6.1.

TRY THIS: Pedagogical Strategy 6.1

Using *Fox* to Interrogate Multiple Perspectives

This is a sophisticated picture book about two characters, Dog and Magpie. Magpie has been wounded and Dog decides to nurse her back to health. Just as their friendship develops, along comes Fox, whom Magpie does not trust, but over time she is persuaded to simulate flying by riding on Fox's back.

Fox takes Magpie far out in the desert and abandons her, telling Magpie that now she too will know what loneliness really feels like. Despite this act of cruelty, the book ends hopefully, as Magpie begins hopping back home.

After orally reading the book, we divide the participants into six groups and ask each group to respond to one of six different stances:

1. **Metaphorical:** Responds by making analogies, or connections, to prior events and life experiences.
2. **Philosophical:** Looks for universal truths or messages that go beyond the text.
3. **Aesthetic:** Responds to the emotional experience of reading; tracks highs and lows during the roller-coaster experience of reading.
4. **Analytical:** Responds to how the text works and why the author wrote it in a particular way; takes a close look at texts and considers why certain words (e.g., characters, settings) were chosen and how they create the effects they do.
5. **Intertextual:** Makes sense of the text in terms of, for example, other texts, movies, or books.
6. **Critical:** Looks for societal stereotypes and patterns or how the text makes us look differently at everyday events; points out the stereotypes that the text perpetuates; helps us see the big issues that lie just beyond the text.

We then ask participants to share the responses they came up with that reflect the stance they were given, and to discuss what kinds of readers are likely to take this kind of stance when responding to texts and which type of responses they think would be the easiest or most natural for them. We also talk about what stances were most challenging and why this might be the case. We then have them reflect on their own experiences in the classroom and the kinds of stances, which were accessible to them as younger learners.

We close this engagement by talking about what is gained by taking on multiple perspectives and by inviting participants to try taking on perspectives they found particularly difficult or unnatural the next time they read a text.

Several secondary teachers with whom we have worked have used the strategy described in Pedagogical Strategy Box 6.1 to re-think and re-configure their high school English classes. While pre-service and in-service teachers often walk away from this engagement understanding that there are multiple ways to respond to a text, it is important to stress that how we respond to text is not only a choice but a responsibility, as our responses reflect how we wish to be positioned in the world and what kind of identity we wish to take on.

Positioning and identity are key dimensions of agency and hence key elements of what it means to take on a critical stance.

Making Multiple Perspectives an Integral Part of the Curriculum

Seeing the world through someone else's eyes is a skill we learn. It cannot be assumed that this is something that most of us pick up on our own. Two of the ways that we continually invite pre-service and in-service teachers to take on multiple perspectives is through the ongoing use of what we describe as "multiview texts" and "text sets."

Multiview Books

Multiview books as described by Lewison et al. (2008) are structured so that characters speak for themselves, often with each page, section, or chapter featuring the perspective or point of view of a different character. Although the characters in these books all experience the same event, their interpretations of the event and their reactions make it clear that they are not coming to the same conclusions. Resource Box 6.1 lists some of the multiview books that we have used in our classrooms as well as the kinds of engagements that lend themselves to working with groups using these books.

RESOURCE BOX 6.1

Mutiview Books for Use in Pre-service and In-service Education

Voices in the Park (Browne 1998)	This text recounts the interactions of two families (one wealthy; one poor) who are at a park at the same time. Groups of students can role play as well as explore the stances, attitudes, and dispositions that are often associated with social class.
Seedfolks (Fleischman, 1997)	Thirteen residents from an inner-city neighborhood respond to an event that happens in a vacant lot near where they live. The book explores how people who have been distrustful of one another might come together for a common purpose. Participants can be assigned one character to describe by unpacking that character's thinking and stance in the world.

From Slave Ship to Freedom Road (Lester, 1998)	A haunting story of slavery which explores the dark, and little thought about, side of slavery. The book invites readers to imagine, via their participation in drama, what it meant to be a slave. Given Rod Brown's powerful art work, participants can be invited to try their own hand at emotionally representing the slave experience.
Under Our Skin: Kids Talk About Race (Birdseye & Birdseye, 1997)	Six 12- and 13-year-olds speak in their own words about their perception of race in America. Participants can be invited to interview a minority youth and write up their story for contribution to a class-composed book.
The Best Part of Me: Children Talk About Their Bodies in Pictures and Words (Ewald, 2001)	Children take pictures of their best features and write about them. Participants can be asked to take pictures of features they like about themselves and explain the genealogy of this feature and its significance.
Making Up Megaboy (Walter, 1998)	A teenager walks into a Korean grocery story and shoots the owner. This incident is explored by a variety of members of the community. Parts can be assigned and participants invited to read their page orally as it comes up in the text.

Text Sets

A text set is a collection of books and other resources that provides many different perspectives on a topic. Since text sets are multimodal, they can include more than just books (Vasquez, 2010). Pictures, videos, songs, maps, diaries, and classroom visitors who have firsthand knowledge of the topic and are willing to share their personal experiences are valuable additions. Experiencing a text set provides multiple perspectives on a topic. What is particularly powerful is that the items in the text set can be used to create space for critical conversation. It is important to remember to include items that contradict or contrast with each other, rather than have all items making the same or a similar point. We often invite pre-service and in-service teachers to create a focused study on a theme of their choice. One aspect of this assignment entails putting together a text set that might be used by students to explore the theme. As part of our introduction to text sets we often bring in a text set we have created and invite participants to look through the text set and note things they find new or interesting on a large sheet of butcher paper we have at that center. Resource Box 6.2 lists a multimodal text set about war that we have created for use in our classes.

RESOURCE BOX 6.2

Text Set on War

Alpha, Bravo, Charlie: The Military Alphabet (Demarest, 2005) *Non-fiction
Eyewitness: Battle (Holmes, 2000) *Non-fiction
Feathers and Fools (Fox, 1989)
Gleam and Glow (Bunting, 2001)
Hisoshima No Pica (Maruki, 1980)
Hiroshima: The Story of the First Atomic Bomb (Lawton, 2004) *Non-fiction
Sadako and the Thousand Paper Cranes (Coerr, 1986)
The Butter Battle Book (Seuss, 1984)
The Cello of Mr. O (Cutler, 1999)
Courtesy of the Red, White, & Blue (Keith, 2004) *Song
Free at last! Stories and Songs of Emancipation (Rappaport, 2004) *Song
On the Bumper of My SUV (Wright, 2004) *Song

REFLECTION POINT 6.1

Creating Text Sets

- What other texts might you add to the text set on war in Resource Box 6.2?
- What topics or issues are on your mind? What texts might you put together to explore those topics or issues?

Extending and Expanding the Meaning of Multiple Perspectives

Teaching, whether with children or adults, has to be up close and personal. The fact that we are not all the same can be used as a resource for exploring the real differences that exist among us. Because so much of our society is grounded in European traditions, values, and beliefs, it is not uncommon for teachers of European ethnic origins to think of themselves as having no culture. Rather than deny our differences—and the privileges or marginalization that goes along with these differences—we need to learn how to use difference as a vehicle for outgrowing our current selves as both individuals and society. One way to begin is by inviting participants to create "A Heritage Museum" as described in Pedagogical Strategy Box 6.2. In this activity participants are asked to bring in three artifacts that represent their various ethnicities or family backgrounds. One artifact should be a book or some type of print material. The other items could include crafts, music, photos, or any number of other mementos. Participants then use these artifacts based on their political, social, and cultural significance in their lives. As Pahl and Rowsell (2010) remind us, "objects come to stand for who they are—their identities" (p. 8).

TRY THIS: Pedagogical Strategy 6.2

Creating a Heritage Museum

- Ask participants to bring in three artifacts (one of which is a book or some type of print material) that represent their various ethnicities or family backgrounds. Other items could include crafts, music, photos, or any number of other mementos.
- Provide each participant a space in the room to create an exhibit with the artifacts that he or she has brought to class.
- Ask participants to think about what is the political, social, and cultural significance of the artifacts they have brought in.
- As students take turns doing a "Gallery Walk" ask them to record things they learned, connections they discovered, or surprises they encountered.
- Ask students to say something regarding issues of diversity and difference, as well as privilege and disadvantage, based on their experience with the Heritage Museum.

No Text is Ever Neutral

One of the key tenets of critical literacy with which we begin is that no text is ever neutral. This means all texts are socially constructed and therefore all texts can be critiqued, examined from different perspectives and then re-constructed or re-designed. It is relatively easy to use Internet search engines to see how different reporters talk about events that affect life in the school communities where pre-service and in-service teachers are likely to be working.

One of the strategies we use to help our students experience the non-neutrality of text is through the use of editorials. After duplicating editorials that address local issues (whether it be teenage curfews at the mall or the dropping of the art and music program in local schools) we ask participants to identify the main issue as well as the various viewpoints expressed. To support their close look at language, we ask them to pay particular attention to instances of language that show which side of the issue a particular author has supported. We close this engagement by discussing whether or not it is possible to be neutral when telling others about an event or is what we see always influenced by what we bring to the situation? We then talk about the ways in which our interpretations of such situations are always mediated through Discourse (ways of being, doing, talking, thinking) and remind them of the importance of identifying the Discourses through which we engage in a situation.

Another strategy that Vivian has used is one she refers to as Blindfolded Readings. What she does is to gather together a variety of junk mail from her mailbox. She then asks for a volunteer who will be blindfolded. She hands this person one piece of junk mail at a time. She then asks the person to give as much information as possible regarding the item in their hand. Volunteers often determine that most of the items are ads or flyers. Vivian then has them talk about what kind of ads and flyers are in their hand and what kinds of items might be pictured on each item. She also has them put in order the pieces of mail based on whether it is associated with inexpensive items or expensive items. With each request, the volunteer readily talks about each of the items placed in their hand based on questions they are asked. The person is then asked to remove the blindfold and look at how accurate their blindfolded readings were.

When Vivian does the Blindfolded Readings participants are always amazed at how accurately they are able to read the texts even when blindfolded. The activity therefore creates a wonderful space for talking about how texts are never neutral and the perspectives we bring to bear on our readings of texts. After all it is our past experiences with particular kinds of ads and flyers that allow us to read such texts even if we cannot see them. Another part of the discussion that follows also focuses on how place or location determines what kinds of ads and flyers end up in the mailbox. More affluent neighborhoods for instance might get in their mailboxes fancy mailings from real estate agents selling expensive homes.

To push the envelope even further we ask participants to talk about how we, as educators, should respond to perspectives that might appear to be potentially hurtful to others. We ask, "Are any perspectives too hot to handle in the classroom?" "Should any be silenced?" Our own research would suggest that there is a direct correlation between a pre-service or in-service teacher believing that their role is to protect the innocence of children and their inability to assume a critical perspective (Albers, Harste, & Vasquez, 2011).

Multiple Perspectives: Some In-process Thoughts

One of the problems with advocating for multiple perspectives is that it sounds too liberal, too politically correct. Everyone believes there are at least two sides to an issue, do they not? What critical educator in his or her right mind would present things as if they were the gospel truth? We argue that even if you buy into the notion of multiple perspectives, it is important to ask the following.

- Why do I hold this belief?
- What is my history behind the perspectives I choose?
- Why are some perspectives more appealing to me than others?
- What are some perspectives I have not explored in the past? Why have I not explored these? What gets in my way? How do I get beyond what gets in the way?
- Where do I think multiple perspectives get us that single perspectives do not?
- How do I ensure that the perspectives I employ are diverse and not rooted in dominant Discourses?

Advocating for multiple perspectives is not unproblematic even for those of us who believe in it. Without a doubt, multiple perspectives complicate what we know and thus complicate curriculum.

Peirce (1931–58), one of America's greatest philosophers, characterized facts as beliefs at rest. By this he meant that things often only look like facts until someone gets up the gumption to study them closely. Given Peirce's insight, our advice is to see no position as right, but rather always look for a third stance, one that disrupts normality (Sumara & Davis, 1999). Curriculum, we believe, is at its best when it teaches against the grain. The key notion underlying multiple perspectives is that there is always more; there is always another stance that needs to be explored. It is this call for "thirdness" that advances thinking.

Have a look at the image labeled Figure 6.1 opposite. It is a watercolor that was initiated by Jerry's five-year-old granddaughter. The initial piece consisted of a blending together of a variety of colors—orange, blue, purple, pink and yellow. When Jerry looked closely at the colors and how they had blended together differently in different areas, he saw a wolf. He then proceeded to add highlights and details to bring the wolf to the surface. This is one way of thinking about a previous statement we made regarding how things often look like facts until someone has the gumption to study them closely and disrupt normality.

Similarly, in selecting materials for pre-service and in-service education, our advice is to seek out engagements that give access to those who have been silenced or marginalized: the migrant farmworker, the unemployed father, the ridiculed child, the genocide victim. Our last bit of advice is to focus all engagements on cooperation rather than competition. In a society such as ours, participants will have had and still get plenty of opportunities to compete with one another. In the pre-service and in-service classroom stress cooperation so students experience the generative potentials of multiple perspectives by working together.

FIGURE 6.1 Wolf.

7

TECHNOLOGY AND MEDIA LITERACY

The history and use of technology and media in the classroom is rich and complex. Teachers have long used media to convey facts and information; however, the form in which it is used is often for entertainment, as a way to reward, rather than for its literary value as noted by a report of the National Council of Teachers of English (NCTE, 2008, para. 1). The growing importance of technology in society has increased what media means for the classroom. NCTE in its position statement about media in the twenty-first century states:

> Because technology has increased the intensity and complexity of literate environments, the twenty-first century demands that a literate person possess a wide range of abilities and competencies, many literacies. These literacies—from reading online newspapers to participating in virtual classrooms—are multiple dynamic and malleable.
>
> *(NCTE, 2008, para. 1)*

REFLECTION POINT 7.1

Literacy Inventory

Use the chart in Figure 7.1 to inventory your literacy activity over the course of a day.

- Column 1—Time and Literacy Activity: Jot down each time you engage in an activity that involves literacy in some way. Make sure to add whether the activity was arts based, print based, etc.

- Column 2—Purpose of Literacy Activity: For each literacy activity note your purpose for having used literacy.
- Column 3—Technology/Media Connection: For each literacy activity note if you used technology or media literacy in some way. Also note what kind of technology or media literacy was used.

At the end of the day, have a look at your inventory and reflect on the following questions:

- What surprised you?
- Did you use media literacy or technology as much as you thought?
- Did you use media literacy or technology as little as you thought?
- How do you use media literacy and technology in your life?

Time and Literacy Activity	Purpose of Literacy Activity	Technology/Media Connection

FIGURE 7.1 Literacy inventory.

In many cases the use of technology has been mandated without offering teachers support in understanding how best to use technology in their settings. Teachers at all levels of education are often given the directive to "incorporate more technology" but what does that really mean for teachers and students? The emergence of media literacy and technology, has helped us to understand that simply seeing literacy as, a "book culture" is not an adequate way to educate students (Luke, 2000, p. 24).

Given the importance of technology in developing literate environments and lives, in this chapter we seek to address what technology and media literacy means for pre-service and in-service teachers in regard to engaging with critical literacies as lived experiences, and the socio-political context often associated with the role of media in schools and society. While we do give suggestions for technology and media use in the classroom, we would have preferred to assume we all understand the implications of what Kellner and Share

(2007) describe as "changes in technology, media, and society that require the development of critical media literacy to empower students and citizens to adequately read media messages and produce media themselves in order to be active participants in a democratic society" (p. 1). However, we realize that in order to use media critically in the classroom, we must be clear on what we see as its importance and the potential "meaning making" affordances it poses for our students such as cultural awareness and an acute understanding of how media impacts our everyday lives.

Shifting Perspectives: Literacy in a Digital and High-tech World

Media literacy in the classroom creates opportunities for students and teachers to examine the socio-political context of literacies that impact their everyday lives and builds on our students' interest in using technology in diverse ways both in and outside of school.

Literacy in a digital and high-tech world, speaks to a shift in perspective or mindset (Kist, 2005; Knobel & Lankshear, 2007; Lankshear & Knobel, 2003). While sharing their view of new literacies, Knobel and Lankshear (2007) identify two interrelated elements: new technical stuff and new ethos. They suggest these two elements are necessary components of work in new literacies. New technical stuff can be employed, to do in new ways, the same kinds of things we have previously known. Equally, however, they can be "integrated into literacy practices that in some significant sense represent new phenomena" (p. 9). In essence, this new technical stuff doesn't just allow us to technologize our existing practice, it creates space for us to move beyond where we are now to allow for greater participation, collaboration, and distribution of knowledge to do things that were not possible with our previous level of technology. Knobel and Lankshear (2007) refer to this as "new ethos stuff." Unlike conventional or expert-dominated literacies, this "new ethos" is "less published, individuated, and authorcentric" (p. 9). Using social media tools like blogs, podcasts, and wikis allows for a broad dispersion of information that is accessible across time and space so that expertise and authority are distributed amongst networks and collectives. The ease and speed with which information can travel seriously disrupts traditional authorial social relations. For instance, Vivian and her husband Andy have been using social media tools for some time. One such tool is Twitter, described as a free social networking and micro-blogging service that allows users to send "updates" (or "tweets"—text-based posts up to 140 characters long) to the Twitter website, via short message service, instant messaging, or a third-party application such as Twitterrific. Updates are then displayed on the user's profile page and instantly delivered to other users who have signed up to receive them. During the Virginia Tech shootings in the spring of 2007, Andy started receiving tweets from Twitter friends in Virginia about what was happening. In fact, as the shootings were taking place, students were using various social media tools to inform one another as to events as they unfolded, which may have kept some students out of harm's way. Gone are the days when newscasts and newscasters held court over the news and what made the headlines. It is no surprise, therefore, to now hear newscasters pointing their audience to their station's podcast or blog site.

Technology-infused Social Practices

When we consider technology-infused social practices, Kress's (2003) idea of "the new page," or the electronic page on a computer screen, identifies for educators possibilities within classroom spaces that encourage multimodality and new literacies, especially as they support students' ability to play with design and create exciting texts. With play comes invention, as students invent new uses for common materials like photos, which can be altered, revised, and enhanced in Photoshop, or video clips that no longer are non-edited streams but involve intentional decisions about moments that are necessary in the viewing and others that can be left "on the cutting floor." Such reflection necessitates a shift in thinking about literacy as more than just a move from a verbal or written expression to a visual or digital expression, but one that considers how identities get positioned in such representations.

In an article on new literacies and technology, Peggy Albers and colleagues state they "… have come to learn that it is not the tools that keep teachers from working with newer literacies; it's the fear that is associated with learning new concepts, software, and ideas and the time it takes to design and develop multimedia projects and shift one's way of thinking" (Albers, Vasquez, & Harste, 2008, p. 5). They further note that what they have learned is that it takes longer to imagine and then carry out the technologization of existing teaching practices and curricular projects than it does to imagine what the new technologies can afford, once that shift in mindset takes place.

The Role of Culture and Cultural Studies

Since its inception, the definition of media literacy has continued to transform. Currently the National Council of Teachers of English defines media literacy as "the capacity to access, analyze, evaluate and communicate messages in a wide variety of forms" (NCTE, 2008, para. 1). Coined in 1964 by John Caulkin, the definition and practice of media literacy continues to evolve and expand as new technology leads to emerging insight about the effects of media on literacy and literacy education (NAMLE, 2007, "Media Literacy," para. 1). Caulkin states:

The attainment of [media] literacy involves more than mere warnings about the effects of the mass media and more even than constant exposure to the better offerings of these media. This [media literacy] is an issue demanding more than good will alone; it requires understanding.

(Moody, 2007, para. 2)

This initial overview of media literacy was for teachers to think in new ways and understand the function of media in culture (Moody, 2007, para. 9). Culkin's original idea establishes the foundation of media literacy—culture. Culture according to Bruner (1996) "takes its inspiration from the evolutionary fact that mind could not exist save for culture" (p. 3) and that "learning and thinking are always *situated* in a cultural setting and always dependent upon the utilization of cultural resources." To understand media literacy one must recognize its apparent and close relationship to culture and cultural studies. According to Giroux (1996):

> Cultural studies, with its ambiguous founding moments spread across multiple continents and diverse institutional spheres, has always been critically attentive to the changing conditions influencing the socialization of youth and the social and economic context producing such changes. The self and social formation of diverse youth subcultures mediated by popular cultural forms remain prominent concerns of cultural studies.
>
> *(p. 15)*

Cultural studies offer a look into the changing conditions that influence the media. Since media is a condition of culture, according to Giroux, we must consider how media such as popular film and music are serious sites for social knowledge but more importantly how the two are inextricably linked.

Additionally, Bruner (1996) offers insight into how culture, "provides us with the toolkit to construct not only our worlds, but our very conceptions of ourselves and our powers" (p. 10). Clearly, media literacy is about the triangulation of culture, power, and identity. Since Bruner sees culture as "a way in which we question about the making and negotiating of meanings [and] about the constructing of self and sense of agency" (p. 12), media literacy is about these same ideological perspectives. According to the National Association for Media Literacy Education (NAMLE) one of the core principles of media literacy is that it recognizes that media is a part of culture and it functions as an agent of socialization. In agreement, Bruner would see culture as key to media literacy because "learning and thinking are always situated in a cultural setting and always dependent upon the utilization of cultural resources." Media literacy relies on culture to provide students with what Luke (2000) states are "critical analytic tools to understand reader and viewer diversity of reading positions and sociocultural locations and differences that influence affinities to particular kinds of media forms and messages"

(p. 425). Additionally, this takes into account Caulkin's initial idea about media literacy requiring "more than good will alone" but a true understanding of the socio-cultural ideas associated with media literacy.

Hall (1999) also presents another overview about how the foundation of media literacy is linked to culture and cultural studies. Media literacy reflects the fluidity of cultural studies. This fluidity is both the intellectual and pragmatic enterprise of media literacy committed to a moral evaluation of modern society and a radical line of political action (Hall, 1999; Sardar & Van Loon, 1998). The same can be said of media literacy with its ever-changing definition due to its roots in culture. Hall asserts that cultural studies are "rooted in a profound tension between ideas of power, global reach, and the history making capacities of capital; the question of class and the complex relationships between power and exploitation" (p. 265). These ideas can be found in the guiding principles of media literacy. One of the principles of media literacy is that it develops "reflective and engaged students that are essential for a democratic society" and that students realize the "socially constructed messages of media." Culture and cultural studies foregrounds media literacy by providing a platform in which to analyze the socio-political nature of media. Finally, Hall asserts that cultural studies have multiple discourses and a number of different histories that speak to media literacy's overall goal to access, analyze, evaluate, and communicate messages in a wide variety of forms (NCTE, 2008, para. 1).

Giroux, Bruner and Hall provide the foundation of media literacy—culture. Each theorist sees culture as a link to defining what media literacy is and forefront the notion that culture encourages students and teachers to reflect and understand the critical and analytical tools to understand positions of power and socio-cultural relations. These theorists provide insight into the notion that media literacy is a site for social knowledge built on the concept that media is a part of culture and a crucial agent in teaching and learning.

Demands of the 21st-century Classroom

According to NCTE, media literacy education may occur as "a separate program or course but often it is embedded within other subject areas, including literature, history, anthropology, sociology, public health, journalism, communication, and education" (NCTE, 2008, para. 1). The content of media literacy can vary from lessons designed to expose the mechanics of how language, images, sound, music, and graphic design operate as a way of transmitting meaning to an exercise designed to reinforce these understandings through hands-on media making (NCTE, 2005, para. 14). We believe that media literacy in the K-12 setting is deeply rooted in the notion that students are more inclined to develop literacy skills if they have a cultural frame that is connected to the material presented during instruction (Duncan-Andrade & Morrell, 2000). Given the belief that students are more inclined to develop literacy skills if they have a cultural frame of reference makes media literacy a necessary tool for the classroom. Additionally, the use of media literacy in the classroom provides different perspectives about what constitutes literacy. Consequently, NCTE advocates broadening the concept of literacy in order for students to apply the knowledge of their language conventions and structure to create, critique and discuss print and non–print texts (NCTE, 2005, para. 10).

Because technology has increased the complexity of what we consider literate environments, the 21st-century classroom demands that students possess a wide range of abilities from reading online articles to participating in virtual classrooms. Currently, most classrooms use some form of media literacy. However, according to Pirie (1997) it is also about changing how literacy is seen in the classroom. More and more there are classroom teachers that effectively use media literacy, not only helping students to become effective users and readers of text but also helping students derive meaning from traditional and canonical texts that are often seen by students as distant and obscure from their everyday lives.

REFLECTION POINT 7.2

Technology Use in the Classroom

What types of technology or media do you use in your classroom? Does media use in your classroom include reading a text and then watching the film associated with that text or do you select or use technology or media that may help your students not only connect to traditional and canonical text but also assist them in "deriving meaning"?

Here are some questions to consider that may assist you in using media with your students:

- What types of technology do you see your students using everyday?
- How does this technology assist students in understanding themselves and those around them? (How and what students use media for (i.e. bullying), can sometimes be more important than the technology itself.) Pay very close attention to what students are using media for.
- How can you incorporate this technology into your lessons in order to assist students in understanding your lesson objectives or make meaning from the assigned text? (i.e. Facebook, Twitter, Blogs). This may take some creativity on your part. You have to research what is popular with students when using these different modalities. Then, use what you know to create lessons that fit with your objectives.

Critical Media Literacy in the Classroom

Inclusion of media literacy in teacher education and K–12 classrooms is not the only issue that we think should be considered when determining media literacy instruction. There is also the issue of "an unprecedented concentration of for-profit media into conglomerates, in alliance with the government and especially with the federal regulating agency—Federal Communications Commission—and other powerful institutions and corporations" (Torres & Mercado, 2006, p. 260). Since media literacy contemplates how "media is constructed" and the "active inquiry and critical thinking of the messages we receive and create," issues of power, privilege and the socio-political context of media within the classroom must be considered.

Torres and Mercado (2006) argue that "corporate culture is taking over public education" (p. 270). While media literacy and education is important, there is still the notion that it must be "critical." Critical should not be viewed as just a "patho-logical response" or negative connotation, but a word that invokes a sense of hope and transformation. So, for this chapter, *critical* articulates the philosophy originally developed by the Frankfurt School. *Critical* presents the belief of empowerment, emancipation, counter-hegemonic discourse and social justice. Kellner and Share (2007) note that "Media and information communication technology can be tools for empowerment when people who are most often marginalized or mis-represented in the main-stream media receive the opportunity to use these tools to tell their stories and express their concerns" (p. 9). They further explain that "for members of the dominant group, critical media literacy offers an opportunity to engage with the social realities that the majority of the world are experiencing" (2007, p. 9). There is a difference here and one that is important to note.

According to Torres and Mercado (2006) one of the dimensions of critical media literacy is "understanding the educators' responsibility to help students become actively engaged in alternative media use and development" (p. 261). While media literacy is crucial, critical media literacy incorporates "the use and abuse of the power of media to control masses of people especially children, for the profit of those who own those media and their political allies" (p. 262). While there is a push for media in the classroom, there are still issues of hegemony and control. Critical media literacy makes explicit the need for alternative media and advises teachers to "help students 'read between the lines' of the media messages, question the interest behind them, and learn how to look for alternative ways to be informed and/or entertained" (p. 273). While the general principles about media literacy defined by NCTE and NAMLE consider some of these aspects, the purposes of critical media literacy according to Torres and Mercado are:

1. To act as intellectual self-defense.
2. To discover and support the increase in number and in power of inde-pendent nonprofit media.

3. To develop alternative media networks among special interest groups using the new advanced media and multimedia technologies and

4. To make information accessible on the democratic premise of education for all.

(p. 278)

Each of these ideas focus on what Torres and Mercado deem "the use and abuse of mass media power by putting profit (economic and political) first and service to the public last" (p. 279). These ideas must also be considered when examining media literacy in the classroom.

Media Literacy in the Teacher Education Classroom

Luke (2000) contends that media, cultural, computer and technology studies can no longer be taught independently of one another (p. 424). She asserts that the development and new framework for media literacy begins in teacher education. Therefore, teacher education programs must provide the necessary tools for teachers to effectively incorporate media literacy into their curriculum.

Luke found that media use in the English Language Arts classrooms had been "reduced to add-on units to more mainstream literary content, or as a remedial strategy to capture reluctant readers or at-risk students for whom traditional literacy instruction has failed" (p. 426). But more importantly she argued that there has been a confinement of media literacy to the English Language Arts classroom thereby reducing media literacy to the teaching of operational skills. In order to address the issue of media literacy in teacher education, Luke believes there are crucial components that must be included in media literacy courses for teachers.

First, there is the issue of multiliteracies (New London Group, 1996). Luke believes multiliteracies should be studied in order to understand how people negotiate their lives using a diversity of literacies (p. 424). Luke argues that because of the many social, political and cultural issues at stake, instruction on the shift from print to cybertextuality is crucial in the education of teachers (p. 427). Luke in her study emphasized the need to move beyond the operational skills of technology and for teachers to understand and reflect on the social and cultural dynamics of teaching in virtual environments. Second, Luke believes that we have to understand issues of technology as it relates to "intercultural communication—that is a heightened meta-awareness (perhaps even self-censorship) of 'others' in our communications ... it is the kind of cultural literacy that is crucial for teachers and students" (p. 432). According to Luke this idea is vital because it requires teachers "to ensure that their students understand concepts of the social and cultural other" (p. 433).

Luke believed these components were important in order to de-emphasize book-based curriculum resources as being the sole source of teaching and learning and a way to "remake" courses on media literacy in teacher education (p. 434). Luke asserts that it is about, "using IT as a tool with which to transform (a) the very relationships between student and teacher, among students, and between students and knowledge and (b) the very organization of school knowledge itself" (p. 435).

Media Literacy in the English Language Arts Classroom

Duncan-Andrade and Morrell (2000) noticed that students who could critically analyze the complex and richly metaphoric and symbolic hip-hop music they listened to were failing to exhibit these same analytical skills when relating to canonical text (p. 2). Their hypothesis was that media literacy or in this case, hip-hop music, could be used as a vehicle for urban youth to develop literary skills. The premise of their argument included the basic notion of media literacy's connection to students' cultural frame of reference, texts that have importance in their lives, in this case hip-hop music, to create and construct meaning from canonical texts.

One of the major principles of media literacy is the idea that students are able to understand how media messages can influence their beliefs, attitudes, values and behaviors in addition to offering students how media is a socialization tool often used to critique and understand society. According to Duncan Andrade and Morrell (2000), hip-hop music is one of the few modes of media that offers a useful approach when using media in the classroom in order to provide cultural and academic relevance to students (p. 24).

Given the intention of media literacy to "access, analyze, evaluate and communicate messages in a wide variety of forms" (NCTE, 2008, para. 1), Duncan-Andrade and Morrell developed what they coined an "intervention project" that would enable students to critique the messages sent to them through a popular cultural medium (rap music) that permeates their everyday life (p. 24). The unit was "designed for both its cultural and academic relevance by incorporating rap music into a poetry unit" (p. 25). In addition to its social and cultural relevance one of the main objectives of this unit was to create a space for urban youth to view elements of popular culture through a critical lens and critique messages sent to them through popular media (p. 25). More importantly, this unit was about using media for literacy development.

The unit started with an overview of poetry and understanding the historical background of poetry for interpretation. For example, Elizabethan, Puritan Revolution, Romantics and Post Industrial Revolution poetry were placed alongside rap music so that students would be able to use a period and genre of poetry they were familiar with as a lens to examine other literary works and re-evaluate the manner in which they view elements of their popular culture (p. 26). After the initial overview of poetry and its relationship to rap music, the second part of the unit was for students to present a poem and rap song. The students prepared interpretations of a chosen poem and rap song with relation to its historical and literary period. For example students matched Walt Whitman's "O Me! O Life!" to the rap group Public Enemy's "Don't Believe the Hype" and Shakespeare's "Sonnet 29" to rapper Nas' "Affirmative Action."

Duncan-Andrade and Morrell's unit was consistent with the ideas of media literacy. The unit provided cultural and social relevancy while exposing students to the literary canon. Additionally, this unit practiced the principles of media literacy because it was situated in the experiences of the students and called for a critical engagement of the text, by asking students to relate it to larger social and political issues. Media literacy calls for these basic tenets. More importantly this unit's use of media enabled students to develop a powerful connection to canonical texts (p. 30).

In addition to the use of rap music in the classroom, other forms of media that are popular within the English Language Arts classrooms provide spaces for students to see literacy in another form. According to Bell (2001), the study of popular culture offers the possibility of understanding how "politics of pleasure" address students in a way that shapes and sometimes secures the often contradictory relations they have to both schooling and the politics of everyday life (p. 241). In this study, Bell looked at how teachers could bring popular film texts into the classroom. Pre-service teachers evaluated and participated in discussions of films in order to develop their use of critical literacy and media the in their classrooms. Critical literacy practices were used with pre-service teachers in order to further their understanding of the possibilities of popular culture. The teachers were not just instructed on the practice of critical literacy, but were also able to experience what it means to critically engage in media literacy for themselves. According to Freebody and Luke (1990), text analysis, or in this case media analysis is a part of what successful readers of media do.

The use of media literacy in the classroom goes beyond the idea of "accessing, analyzing and evaluating communicate messages." Media literacy in the classroom is about how this practice can transform students and teachers not just socially and politically, but academically as well.

REFLECTION POINT 7.3

Media Literacy Previously Explored

Revisit Chapters 4, 5, and 6 in this book. What are some ways that media literacy is explored in those chapters?

TRY THIS: Pedagogical Strategy 7.1

Creating a Multimedia Text Set

Multimedia text sets provide a powerful space to get at the notion that texts are never neutral and that they are always created from particular perspectives to convey certain messages. Multimedia text sets include texts created using other sign systems such as paintings, sculptures, movies, and music. A sign system is a way of representing meaning using different materials (media such as paint and clay) and ways of communicating (media such as a painting, video, or sculpture). Each text in the set can be used to read the others in the set. For instance, as a way of better understanding or talking about the issues in *White Wash* (Shange, 1997), the book could be combined with other texts that reflect similar issues. These could be texts that offer an alternate or counter take on the issue or that complement the issue. Each text can then be used as a lens, framework, or perspective to read the others.

In her book *Getting Beyond I Like the Book: Creating Spaces for Critical Literacy in K-6 Settings* (Vasquez, 2010), Vivian shares an example of a multimedia text set focused on power, control, and positioning. The set includes the picture book *White Wash* (Shange, 1997) and art work created by artists from the stolen generation of Australia. The "stolen generation" refers to the Aboriginal people of Australia who were taken from their families as young children to breed the Aborigine out of them. In essence, this was a way to make them white, as was the case with the racial incident experienced by Helene-Angel in *White Wash* (Shange, 1997). Pamela Croft, an Aboriginal Australian artist, is one of the stolen generation. Included in the text set is a documentary of Croft's life called *Back to Brisbane*. Other texts that Vivian included were a Stolen Generation Timeline and The Northern Territory of Australia Aboriginal Ordinance 1918, which resulted in Aboriginal children being taken from their families and placed in special reserves. An image of the primary document of this ordinance can be viewed at the National Library of Australia website (nla.gov.au/nla.aus-vn1949075-2x).

This multimedia text set provides spaces for rich discussion about issues of power, control, and positioning.

- Make a list of the topics of interest shared by the pre-service and in-service teachers with whom you work.
- Choose one of the topics and begin to build a multimedia text set to support exploration of that topic.
- What texts did you include in your set?
- How did the use of multimodal texts enrich your conversations and learning about a particular topic?

TRY THIS: Pedagogical Strategy 7.2

The Soundtrack of Our Lives

As teacher educators, we often encounter questions on how to incorporate media or technology into the classroom. A strategy that Stacie uses is to assist her pre-service teachers with not only incorporating media in the classroom, but also assisting her pre-service teachers on to create meaning through a particular media modality such as music.

We know that music can tell a story sometimes better than the written word. However, we also know that music brings words to life. Music continues to be a powerful medium for society and a particularly powerful one for students. If this is the case, how can we include this media in the classroom? Following is an example of one way to do just that.

If you could tell your story in music, what tracks would you use? Would you be able to characterize who you are in ten songs or less? Using Internet applications such as Pandora or your own music library, come up with the soundtrack that best describes who you are. This exercise will help you understand and derive meaning about the idea of characterization.

- Choose ten songs.
- Explain why each of these songs characterizes who you are. You not only have to choose the song, but you have to explain why that particular song speaks to who you are.
- Once you have developed your own soundtrack, what soundtrack would you choose for characters that you are discussing in your classroom? For example, what soundtrack would you choose in order to describe the relationship between Shakespeare's Romeo and Juliet?
- What soundtrack would you choose to describe a character like Jay Gatsby from *The Great Gatsby*? You can choose any song that you like but you must be able to rationalize its use, so be careful with your selections.
- Discuss.

The DC Area Literary Map Podcast

In Vivian's work creating spaces for critical literacies with young children, she has maintained that a critical literacy curriculum needs to be lived as an overarching transgressive perspective or stance that is fluid and that should be reoriented depending on the context within which teachers and students find themselves (Vasquez et al., 2003; Vasquez, 2004). While working with her teacher education students, therefore, she makes it clear to them that the projects they take on in the university classroom are demonstrations of possibilities that can serve as resources for imagining critical literacy projects in their own settings.

One such project, is the DC Area Literary Map Podcast. Vivian came up with this project after listening to students in her children's literature courses talk about ways in which they use books in the classroom, their choice of books for their students, and their struggle over finding books that connected to their students' lives in some way.

A podcast is an Internet-based audio or video broadcast that is downloadable to a computer or onto an MP3 player. (MP3 is the standard format for encoding audio for Internet broadcast, and an iPod is one example of such a player.) Podcasts are created by digitally recording audio using any one of a range of digital recording devices such as the i-River or ZoomH2; these recorders automatically digitize audio by recording in MP3 format. Some podcasters record directly onto their computers, using software such as Audacity or Garage Band, which can also be used to edit recorded audio. This would be the point at which music and sound effects are added. Once audio is recorded and put in an MP3 format, it is then uploaded to an online host. Popular inexpensive web hosts include Libsyn (http://www.libsyn.com) and GoDaddy (http://www.godaddy.com). Once uploaded on a host server, the audio location is added to an RSS feed, which is what people subscribe to in order to download a podcast to their computers and then to MP3 players. Since first attempting this project, Vivian has tried different ways of producing the audio, from setting aside recording time during class to having students create audio on their own.

Finding books that connect to the world in which their students live was an issue that seemed to come up for Vivian's pre-service teachers semester after semester, year after year. She came up with the DC Area Literary Map Podcast idea as one way to help them become more resourceful when it came to choosing books for their students. She also wanted to create a project that could be useful beyond the immediate needs of her students. Finally she wanted to create a project that could be generative, ongoing, and sustainable beyond the life of the course. Vivian has assigned different iterations of the project over the last two years, each one representing her attempts at refining and re-framing the project in hopes of better clarifying what it means to frame the work from a critical literacy perspective. With each new group of teachers, the map has grown, and it has become a more useful and interesting resource for teachers in the DC area who want to explore the use of multimodal text sets. Listeners to the podcasts are able to comment on and contribute to what could be an ongoing conversation about particular texts, issues, and topics. The project is located at http://www.bazmakaz.com/lit_map_dc/lit_map_dc.html.

To get this assignment going students are told that they are to create a four-minute audio or video recording to be added to a literary map podcast of the DC area (see Figure 7.2). As part of their multimodal reading list, which includes

A LITERARY MAP PODCAST ~ THE WASHINGTON DC AREA

CREATED BY CLASSROOM TEACHERS

CLICK HERE
TO ACCESS
THE MAP   Washington, D.C.

FIGURE 7.2 Literary map.

podcasts, blogs, and other Internet texts, Vivian has them familiarize themselves with the project by spending some time exploring a the project website.

She explains to them that over the years, literary maps have been used to help students and readers learn about literature, writers, and places, and that in a way, these maps help to bring to the surface the social construction of the texts they represent by geographically locating characters and storylines, and historicizing them. She then has them listen to examples of podcasts that represent the kind of multimedia text set audio they will be creating. These include the following, all found on www.clippodcast.com: Acts of Kindness and Social Action, CLIP 23; Acts of Courage and Acts of Kindness, CLIP 16; A Crossover Show with JOMB on Elbert's Dad Word, CLIP 12; Multi-media Text Set, CLIP 3.

To create their audio, teachers begin by reading a book that disrupts a social issue (e.g., racism, bullying, sexism, homophobia). The issue they choose is meant to reflect their own students' inquiry questions. Vivian tells them that the text they choose should connect in some way to the DC area so that we can "map it." She then asks them to locate a public monument or setting (in the DC area) and a poem, song, art piece, or *movie* that enriches the reading of the original text. Once they have the pieces they need, the teachers begin crafting a description of their text set from a critical literacy perspective. Since for many of the teachers, this is their first introduction to critical literacy, the scripts they create for the map are not always critical, but Vivian values their attempts as opportunities for them to begin to imagine what it means to work within a critical literacy framework.

In a lot of ways, the work represents attempts at creating spaces for critical literacies. The use of multiple texts that address the same issue or topic is meant to help students to further understand that texts are never neutral, which is why they engage in analytically unpacking the words and images in them. As part of creating the narrative for their contribution, they are meant to unpack both language and image choices in those texts, consider how these texts position them as readers, as well as the position from which they engage with the texts and construct meaning from them. The students are asked to work from the premise that reading children's literature involves the active process of predicting and confirming, or revisiting their hypothesis about the words and images on the page based on their own past experiences, and that it is by no means a passive process of decoding words and information. More specifically, they discuss how texts are constructed, by whom, and for what purpose(s). They also talk about ways that the texts advantage some while disadvantaging others by foregrounding particular themes and "back-grounding" others. Further, Vivian also helps them to understand what it means to unpack the positions and stances from which texts are written and consumed, including the use of new technologies such as podcasting. Beyond this, the rest is up to their creativity. In addition to creating their audio, Vivian asks her students to create a collage that represents their focal issues or topics.

To listen to the podcasts, a listener can either click on a numbered point on the DC area map (see Figure 7.3), after which time an image (the collage) pops up and the audio automatically plays, or the listener can go to the podcast homepage and click on the audio symbol included in each posted episode. Those interested could also subscribe to the podcast using media tools such as iTunes in order to receive new shows automatically when they are released.

One of Vivian's student's began her podcast with a discussion of book banning and the influence of the Christian Right. She says.

> *Politics and children's literacy seem to be two areas of thought which are incompatible. Politics being the administration of power and control, and children's literature: the freedom of imagination. However, embedded political perspectives, whether religious, social, or gender based, affect the selection and availability of children's literature.*
>
> *The Christian Right exercises massive political power in the United States. President George W. Bush has given the Christian Right a significant voice in shaping positions on a lot of issues. Many conservative judges have been appointed and exercise leadership with the Congress in passing legislation that is defined by biblical norm regarding family, sexuality, freedom of speech and I would add freedom of reading.*
>
> *This is why on the map, I chose the United States Capitol. It is the Capital building that serves as the seat of government for the United States Congress. It is located on top of Capitol Hill at the east end of the National Mall. The building is marked by its central dome and two wings: one for each chamber of Congress. The north wing is the Senate and the south wing is the House of Representatives. According to some GOP members of the Congress traditional family values have been under attack for the past 40 years. Apparently the problem is Hollywood, the music industry, and certain books. Society needs to be saved from moral destruction and the minds of the children need to be protected.*

Literary Links

To access literary audio, click the links on the left or the numbered hot spots on the map.
Podcast link coming soon!

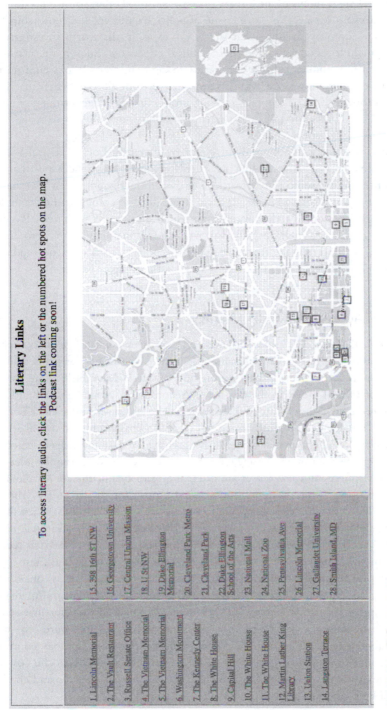

1. Lincoln Memorial
2. The Vault Restaurant
3. Russell Senate Office
4. The Vietnam Memorial
5. The Vietnam Memorial
6. Washington Monument
7. The Kennedy Center
8. The White House
9. Capital Hill
10. The White House
11. The White House
12. Martin Luther King Library
13. Union Station
14. Langston Terrace

15. 598 16th ST NW
16. Georgetown University
17. Central Union Mission
18. 1i St NW
19. Duke Ellington Memorial
20. Cleveland Park Metro
21. Cleveland Park
22. Duke Ellington School of the Arts
23. National Mall
24. National Zoo
25. Pennsylvania Ave
26. Lincoln Memorial
27. Gallaudet University
28. Smith Island, MD

FIGURE 7.3 DC area map.

She then briefly discusses the history of censorship and offers some texts through which to gain perspective on the issue of politics, children, and censorship. She ends her audio by sharing what she refers to as "paths worth investigating." These include social issues and their political effects on children, the nature of the publishing industry, marketing trends, foreign children's books (and related language and cultural translation issues), the freedom allowed when matching illustrations with text, independent book production units, government reading lists, school library funding, and the lack of ability for children to make their own reading selections.

For this student, thinking about children's literature from a critical-literacy perspective created space for her to articulate and make public issues that had been brewing for some time. Hearing her own thoughts on the air gave her an opportunity to further unpack her own ideologies and come to a better understanding of the stances and positions from which she engages with texts. Reading and reacting to comments by others provided additional opportunities to discuss the issue at hand, thereby further helping the podcast reader/listener/audience make informed decisions about their stance on the topic or issue.

Equity, Access and Media Literacy

While media literacy is an important trend that many educators and researchers believe is necessary to create multiliterate students, the reality for many students and schools is that standardized testing and resources leave little room for the incorporation of media in the classroom. According to Noguera (2008), NCLB has forced many schools to eliminate subjects like art, music and science because they are not covered on standardized test (p. 179). If basic subjects such as art and science are being eliminated where does that leave media and media instruction? Many schools continue to struggle for basic resources. New textbooks, adequate school resources and test scores are often the priority, not the use of media in the classroom. While there continues to be a push for media literacy there is still a "digital divide." In a study conducted by Hess and Leal (2001) they found that students in districts with a larger percentage of African-American students had less access to classroom computers. Additionally, since urban districts receive most of their funding for technology initiatives from federal funds, test scores attached to federal dollars means that under-achieving schools miss out on the funding necessary to address media and technology needs (p. 766). If media literacy argues that students must be "reflective and engaged participants essential for a democratic society" there must be initiatives in place to ensure "equitable and substantial access" to media (p. 766). While the role of technology continues to become a pressing issue, there is still the matter of access. With the cost and complexity of new technologies, how can we ensure that effective and efficient media literacy is provided to all students?

Digital Technologies and Empowered Literacy Learning

With the growing field of technology, media literacy continues to evolve. NCTE and others have continued to ensure that media literacy includes "both receptive and productive dimensions, encompassing critical analysis and communication skills, particularly in relationship to mass media, popular culture and digital media" (NCTE, 2008, para. 1). Subsequently, this evolvement has not always considered the cultural and political conventions of society. While the evolution of media literacy continues to grow it must do so with issues of power, access and privilege in mind. For this chapter media literacy is more than the capacity to "access, analyze, evaluate and communicate messages." Media literacy gives students and teachers the opportunity to examine the socio-political context of literacies that impact their everyday lives.

We live in a highly wired and visually sophisticated world. As teacher educators we need to re-conceptualize teacher education so as to include engagements that allow teachers to discover for themselves the relationship between digital technologies and empowered literacy learning. Teachers, after all, can only do for students what they have experienced for themselves. If we wish to create individuals who are critically literate, it is important that students not only experience a variety of communicative tools but do so across the curriculum and in a way that allows them to deal with issues of social significance. So while English language arts teachers need to explore the potential of technology to communicate, they also have to critically study how such media shapes viewers' interpretations. To be fully literate is to take social action by actively deciding how you wish to position yourself in the world and what identity you wish to take on.

RESOURCE BOX 7.1

Media Literacy and Technology Resources

Gee, J.P. (2007). *What video games have to teach us about learning and literacy* (2nd ed.). New York, NY: Palgrave Macmillan.

Kellner, D. & Share, J. (2007). Critical media literacy, democracy, and the reconstruction of education. In D. Macedo & S.R. Steinberg (Eds.), *Media literacy: A reader* (pp. 3–23). New York: Peter Lang Publishing.

Macedo, D. & Steinberg, S.R. (Eds.) (2007). *Media literacy: A reader*. New York, NY: Peter Lang Publishing.

Marsh, J. (Ed.) (2005). *Popular culture, new media and digital literacy in early childhood*. London, UK: Routledge.

Marshall, E. & Sensoy, O. (Eds.) (2011). *Rethinking popular culture and media.* Milwaukee, WI: Rethinking Schools.

Vasquez, V. (2010). *Getting beyond I like the book: Creating spaces for critical literacy in K-6 classrooms* (Chapter 3, pp. 39–53). Newark, DE: International Reading Association.

Vasquez, V. & Felderman, C. (2013). *Technology and critical literacy in early childhood.* New York, NY: Routledge.

8

TEACHING AND LIVING CRITICAL LITERACIES

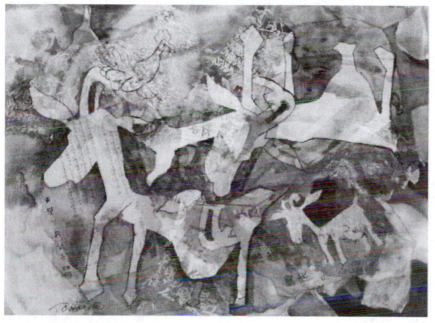

Jerome C. Harste
(Bloomington, IN)

Inscribed Goats
Watercolor collage 12"x16" 2010

FIGURE 8.1 Inscribed goats.

Jerry

I think ever since I encountered Picasso's She-Goat at the Modern Museum of Art (MoMA) in New York City I have been in love with goats. Like Picasso who created his She-Goat out of pieces of metal and shards of ceramics that potters had thrown in the field next to his studio, this collage is made of pages of English and Chinese text on top of a discarded attempt at painting a close-up of flowers (that is where the original colors came from and one of the elements that gives the painting unity). To complete the work I made a stencil and a rubber stamp of a sketch of Picasso's goat I had drawn in my journal at the time I visited the MoMA in 2008. I drew goats upside down and all around the painting as well as stenciled in several smaller goats.

A viewer later asked me if I had drawn the goats to suggest "death" as that was what several artists in history had done. I had to admit that while I liked this "reading," it was not what I had intended.

The message I was attempting to get across was that we are inscribed with literacy and as such we (globally) have been "goats" to the very texts that both create us and give us our identity. My upside-down goats were simply meant to suggest that our goat-like behavior be looked at from the other side. At the last minute I threw in a chicken just to give viewers a reason to take a second, closer, look.

Living a critically literate life is not easy. It is not easy because for the most part so many of us have been as Jerry noted in his painting "goats to the system" or as he writes " 'goats' to the very texts that both create us and give us our identity." It is not until we take stock of the positions from which we live our lives, take a step back and look at our "goat-like" behavior from different perspectives that we are able to figure out alternative life paths and ways of being. Doing so is important.

In Chapter 3 we presented a teacher whose philosophy became his anchor. Being able to name the ideologies he embodied and the Discourses through which he lived his life helped him to better articulate why he did what he did in terms of his teaching practice. We believe his critical perspective worked to create a space for him to negotiate a classroom that reflected his beliefs about education. It should be noted that this did not happen for him overnight. It took years of work and is still an ongoing process as it should be. What is clear is that he lives his theory. If there is one message we want you to take away from reading this book it is to remember the importance of living your theory. We are talking about living a critically literate life as discussed several times throughout this text. Doing so would require us to turn our goats upside down, disrupt normalized dominant often inequitable ways of being and maybe even "throw in a chicken" as Jerry suggested in order to help us to take another look—a closer look toward change.

In some ways becoming a goat to the system happens because as Campano (2012) reminds us shedding our cultures and identities is systemically hardwired into the institution of school. While critical literacy and critical pedagogy may seem like a challenge, heeding Campano's (2012) message is an important step in participating in the dance of critical literacy.

In Chapters 4, 5, and 6 we offered strategies for you to look more closely at society, your students, and most importantly yourself as one way to further explore what it means to practice what you preach. Doing so also requires a keen understanding of your students and school community. It requires understanding by unpacking your own biases and your own privileges. We must begin to critically assess who we are as educators, what we believe and how that unfolds within our classrooms and our personal lives. One way to do this is through the use of biographical narratives that help us to unpack our buried histories and experiences or those histories we sometimes unknowingly overlook. In keeping with our belief of walking our talk following are Stacie's and Jerry's narratives.

Stacie

When people ask how I decided to become a teacher and researcher, I always reply, "I was groomed for this." My life from the moment of conception has been a cycle of love and commitment from complete strangers to family and friends. As a result, it has brought me to the life that I now lead. Love, commitment and benevolence have been the cornerstone of my existence. I am adopted. I was given up two months after my birth. According to the records, my birth mother actually kept me for two months then decided that she could no longer take care of me. I spent roughly four months in a foster home then was adopted by my parents. Before the age of one, the cycle of love began. I had at least two caregivers (my birth mother and foster mother) who undoubtedly loved and took care of me—one who was a mother the other a total stranger.

Over the last twenty years my work has focused on the need to understand and improve the learning opportunities for students of color in urban areas. This philosophy, I believe, is in direct correlation with my own background and my family's educational history. In examining my own story, I began to understand how issues like being a first-generation college student and the implications that this label (remember the importance of labels in Chapter 3) had on my academic development. In society's eyes, I was a first-generation college student who would probably not attend college let alone receive a doctorate because of my parents' educational history. I believe this has driven my overall educational philosophy about improving the opportunities for students of color and first-generation college students. I believe this philosophy is deeply rooted in my own teaching and research.

Part of why I became a teacher and researcher was to create opportunities for students. I wanted to know what practices were improving the academic success of students of color. More importantly, I believe that my overall philosophy about education takes into account that as a teacher and researcher, I wanted to understand the vast body of knowledge about what works in education. I wanted to ensure that I and other students of color were able to change and challenge the perceptions of first-generation college students and what we are able to achieve.

From teaching high school English, to becoming a college administrator who helped under-represented students attend and navigate higher education, my goal in each of these situations has always been equity, social justice and a pedagogy of caring. I believe my search for social justice started in high school. I vividly remember taking part in a student protest in order to receive the same programs as a neighboring school. I grew up knowing the results of inequity but nothing like I see in the schools that I work in now.

My personal narrative also reveals my frustration with an inequitable educational system. My current research explores the use of critical literacy and critical pedagogy as practices that can create a significant change for students of color. Because of my background, I believe my research is about praxis—praxis for my students, and for those in my own life. Each of my educational experiences has provided a way for me to give back. The love and care that has been shown to me by family, community members and complete strangers has pushed my research and pedagogy. This push is one that advocates for change in the way that we view others and ourselves. I believe my adoption spearheaded how I view my place in the world. I have always had the need to give back to a world that has provided me with so much. With each class I teach or research project I conduct, a guiding factor is the love and understanding that I have of others and the need to make a difference. Is living a critically literate life difficult? Yes. But it is a difficulty that I take on willingly.

Jerry

I often say that for the first 16 years of my life I attended church six nights a week. One of the most liberating events that ever happened to me was going to college. While I turned my back on organized religion, certain values, like community, problem solving, taking initiative, and not following the flock remained important to me. You will see these values at play in many of the decisions I made in the 60s and 70s, including joining the Peace Corps and protesting the Viet Nam War. One of the things my stint in the Army taught me is to never give up on your values. While I spoke out against the Viet Nam War, when push came to shove, I decided I would rather be inducted than be a draft dodger. The two years I spent in the Army were the two worst years of my life. On a daily basis I found myself engaged in actions I didn't believe in. I decided if I ever got out I would never deliberately violate my most fundamental beliefs every again. Throughout the 80s, 90s, and 2000s I have been an advocate of whole language, inquiry-based learning, multiple ways of knowing and critical literacy. Underlying each of these movements is the fundamental set of values I learned from growing up in a tightly knit German farming community—the belief that each individual can make a difference, the importance of critique, the importance of walking the walk as well as talking the talk, the importance of inquiry, the importance of alternate perspectives, the betterment of life for generations to come.

Inside–Outside Art

Another strategy is the use of art (See Figures 8.2 and 8.3). Jerry and Vivian did a workshop with teachers in the summer of 2012 where they had the teachers create representations of what they referred to as their inside and outside self. This work was based on the book *Just Like Me: Stories and Self-Portraits by Fourteen Artists* by Harriet Rohmer (1997).

Participants were first asked to bring artifacts that say something about them. To start they shared their artifacts with one another. Pahl and Rowsell (2010) note that "identities reside on a sea of stuff and experiences" (p. 8). While sharing participants unpacked that "stuff" and their experiences. They were then asked to create a self-portrait to be placed at the center of their art piece. They used conversations, topics, and issues that came up during their discussion to inform the creation of their art.

Some people created sketches and watercolor portraits while others embellished photographs of themselves. The image on the left side of Figure 8.3 was done using watercolors and permanent marker while the image on the right was created using a photograph, markers and paint. Around the self-portrait participants were asked to place words and images or artifacts that represent who they are on the inside and who they are on the outside.

Following is what participants were asked to consider when choosing text, images and artifacts for their outside self:

1. How does your artifact reflect how you see yourself as having been positioned by people, places, institutions…around you?
2. What are words or phrases that would represent #1?
3. How might you represent your artifact(s) visually while accounting for your response to #1 and #2?

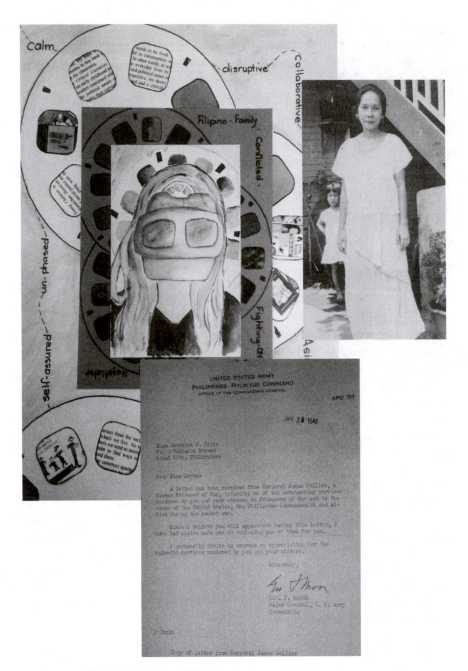

FIGURE 8.2 Vivian's inside–outside art.

FIGURE 8.3 Inside–outside art.

Following is what participants were asked to consider when choosing text, images and artifacts for their inside self.

1. How does your artifact represent "the inside" you?
2. How does this artifact represent how you see yourself and the identities that you try to embody?
3. What words or phrases could you use to represent #1 and #2?
4. How might you represent your artifact visually while accounting for your response to #1, #2, and #3?

The examples in Figure 8.3 show how differently participants approached the activity. The person on the left used a variety of artifacts (maps) and images (photographs) and a few words. The person on the right used primarily words cut out from magazines with a few images also cut out from magazines.

As a culminating experience we put on a museum display whereby all participants were able to showcase and share their creations alongside their artifacts. Vivian tried her hand at this inside-outside art as well. Figure 8.2 is the piece she created to represent herself.

Vivian

I brought three artifacts to represent me—two letters and a photograph. One letter was written in 1946 and the other in 1948. The photo was taken in 1942 (see Figure 8.2) and it depicts my Grandmother and my aunt who was about 8-years-old at the time the photo was taken. These artifacts were given to me after my aunt passed away a few years ago. The letter written in 1948 was from the Office of the Commanding General of the United States Army Philippines Ryukyus Command. It was addressed to my Grandmother's older sister, Miss Severina G. Reyes.

Dear Miss Reyes,
A letter has been received from Corporal James Collier, a former Prisoner of War informing me of the outstanding services rendered by you and your sisters to Prisoners of War and to the cause of the United States, the Philippine Commonwealth and Allies during the recent war.

Since I believe you will appreciate having this letter, I have had copies made and am enclosing one of them for you.

I personally desire to express my appreciation for the splendid services rendered by you and your sisters.

Sincerely,
GEO F. Moore
Major General, US Army Commanding

I had absolutely no idea my family had aided the American soldiers in the Philippines during the time known as the Japanese invasion. What struck me was that my family had sacrificed their lives for the soldiers even though in the past the Philippines had been annexed by the USA and then abandoned to fend for itself.

I am often asked how I became interested in critical literacies but until these letters surfaced I had no idea that fighting for justice was part of my legacy. Somehow family members of my grandparents' generation had managed to keep this history tucked away in their memories.

When it came time to create my portrait I decided to paint an image of myself with a Viewmaster in front of my eyes. I remember having one of those Viewfinders as a child. The slides were not labeled so I never knew what I was going to see next. I decided this would be one way to represent the surprise discovery of the letters. Covering my face also represents the jostling of my identities having discovered a familial history that I was not aware of and yet that is in keeping with the work that I do today.

To represent my outside self I decided to create large versions of the Viewmaster slides. I then made copies of pages from some of my publications along with small images of my book covers. I had these printed on acetate to mimic the slide film. I then cut the acetate images to the shape of the square images on the large Viewmaster slide. Following this I printed words like un-phased, Asian, flexible, and collaborative around the outside border of the piece to represent how I felt those around me positioned me in life.

For my inside self I created smaller slide wheels and then copied the letter and photograph onto acetate sheets. I then cut these up to represent the square pieces on the slide wheel. My inside words included words such as Filipino, conflicted and fighting on.

Pahl and Rowsell (2010) tell us that artifacts can help us to tell "new kinds of stories" (p. 8), that help shape for us, new identities. This certainly has been the case for me. I now feel as though I have to re-think how I position myself as a critical literacy educator. And the next time someone asks me about where I cut my critical literacy teeth, I will have new stories to tell.

Dealing with Accountability and Standards

A question that often arises for us is how to get beyond the hurdles of incorporating a critical stance when we live in a world of accountability and standards. We understand why some may feel concerned. However, we have found that these difficulties become easier with teachers who have a concrete philosophy about their pedagogy and can demonstrate how this type of pedagogy has changed their own academic and personal lives as well as that of their students.

We have also found that you cannot do this work alone. Having others to think with and reflect with, even if they are not in your workplace makes all the difference in whether you continue to create more and more spaces for critical literacy in your setting or whether you throw in the towel. This is why we advocate for the teacher–researcher model. It is not enough to say that you practice critical literacy; you have to demonstrate the possibilities it creates for your students.

This type of pedagogy places stock in humanity and the good that can occur when we realize that our struggle for humanity is a "conquest not a gift" (Friere, 1970). While many people think that we live in a so-called "post-racial" society, the reality is that this post-racial idea has illuminated how much more vigilant we need to be against oppression, racial and gender discrimination as well as the inequitable class structure. We believe that this "post-racial" definition is a call for us as teachers and educators to understand the world around us and to live a life that reveals what the post-racial definition conceals—the pervasive inequalities within our society.

In Chapter 7 we presented a concrete definition of media studies and technology with the intention of demonstrating how media can be used to mediate critical literacies in the classroom. Key tenets of this chapter promoted the idea that media can and should reflect the lived experiences of our society and our students. We also examined how media can create meaning for our students by using a medium that is a part of their everyday life. Media studies and technology within a "critical literacy as a lived experience" framework begins to unlock how technology can be used as a modality that offers "serious sites for social knowledge (Giroux, 1996).

Critical Literacy as Social Practice

Pre-service and in-service teachers need to understand that a critical stance entails taking on a set of key attitudes and dispositions, which we have talked about in Chapters 2 and 4. Teaching from a critical perspective does not entail introducing particular topics or focusing on particular issues but rather involves putting in place a set of social practices that invite students to live critically.

Inherent in this line of thinking—just as with anything else we do in classrooms—are a set of assumptions that continually need to be questioned. One evaluative question that a critical educator needs constantly to be asking is: "To what extent do the engagements I select in my classroom support the taking on of multiple perspectives for purposes of disrupting commonplace knowledge, including my own?" Posing this question forces us to confront uncertainty (MacGinitie, 1983; Harste, 2008b), and reminds us that critical literacy needs to begin at home, with us, with our students, with what we know.

When methods are seen as sets of social practice rather than as materials and procedures, methods do make a difference (Harste, 2008a). In a sense, one has to look beyond the surface level of engagements to the larger social practices that are being put in place. Whatever we are teaching at this moment is just one particular engagement; just one instance of a social practice we are trying to put in place. From this perspective, the curricular engagements that we have introduced in this book are best seen as a starter kit. Therefore it will be up to you to build your repertoire of practice that helps you to negotiate critical literacies that makes sense in your own setting.

REFLECTION POINT 8.1

What are some ways that you might negotiate critical literacies in your setting?

REFERENCES

Albers, P. (2007). *Finding the artist within: Creating and reading visual texts in the English language arts classroom*. Newark, DE: International Reading Association.

Albers, P., Harste, J.C., Vander-Zanden, S. & Felderman, C. (2008). Using popular culture to promote critical literacy practices. In Y. Kim, V. Risko, D. Compton, D. Dickinson, M. Hundley, R. Jimenez, K. Leander, & D. Rowe (Eds.), *57th Yearbook of the National Reading Conference* (pp. 70–83). Oak Creek, WI: NRC.

Albers, P., Harste, J.C., & Vasquez, V. (2010). *I'm risking it! Teachers take on consumerism*. Presentation given at the Annual Meeting of the Literacy Research Association, Austin, TX.

Albers, P., Harste, J.C., & Vasquez, V. (2011). Interrupting certainty and making trouble: Teachers' written and visual responses to picturebooks. In P.J. Dunston, L.B. Gambrell, K. Headley, S.K. Fullerton, P.M. Stecker, V.R. Gillis, & C.C. Bates (Eds.), *60th Yearbook of the Literacy Research Association* (pp. 179–194). Oak Creek, WI: LRA.

Albers, M., Vasquez, V. & Harste, J. (2008). A classroom with a view: Teachers, multi-modality and new literacies. *Talking Points, 19*(2), 3–13.

Albers, P., Vasquez, V., & Harste, J.C. (2011). Making visual analysis critical. In D. Lapp & D. Fisher (Eds), *The handbook of research on teaching the English language arts.* (pp. 195–201). Mahwah, NJ: Routledge-LA.

Altwerger, B. & Strauss, S.L. (2002). The business behind testing. *Language Arts, 49*(3), 256–262.

Anderson, M.T. (2012). *Feed*. Sommerville, MA: Candlewick Press.

Anyon, J. (1997). *Ghetto schooling: A political economy of urban educational reform*. New York: Teachers College Press.

Ball, D. (1993). With an eye on the mathematical horizon: Dilemmas of teaching elementary school mathematics. *Elementary School Journal, 93*, 373–397.

Bartolome, L. (2003). Beyond the methods fetish: Toward a humanizing pedagogy. In Darder, et al. (Eds.), *The critical pedagogy reader* (p. 263). New York, NY: Routledge Falmer.

Bell, J. (2001). Building bridges/making meanings: Texts of popular culture and critical pedagogy in theory and practice. In B. Comber & A. Simpson (Eds.), *Negotiating critical literacies in classrooms* (pp. 229–244). Mahwah, NJ: Lawrence Erlbaum Associates.

Birdseye, D. & Birdseye, T. (1997) *Under our skin: Kids talk about race.* New York, NY: Holiday House.

Boler, M. & Zembylas, M. (2003). Comforting truths: The emotional terrain of understanding difference. In P.P. Trifonas (Ed.), *Pedagogies of difference: Rethinking education and social change* (pp. 110-136). New York: Routledge.

Booth, W. (1988). *The company we keep: An ethics of fiction.* Berkley, CA: California University Press.

Boston Weatherford, C. (2007). *Freedom on the menu.* New York, NY: Puffin Books.

Bourdieu, P. (1986). The forms of capital. In J.G. Richardson (Ed.), *Handbook of theory and research for the sociology of education* (pp. 241–258). New York: Greenwood Press.

Browne, A. (1998). *Voices in the park.* New York, NY: DK Publishing.

Browne, A. (2000). *Willy & Hugh.* London, UK: Red Fox.

Browne, A. (2004). *Into the forest.* Sommerville, MA: Candlewick.

Bruchac, J. (2004). *Hidden roots.* New York, NY: Scholastic.

Bruner, J. (1996). *The culture of education.* Cambridge, MA: Harvard University Press.

Buck, P. & Sylvester, P.S. (2005). Preservice teachers enter urban communities: Coupling funds of knowledge research and critical pedagogy in teacher education. In N. Gonzalez, L.C. Moll & C. Amanti (Eds.), *Funds of knowledge: Theorizing practices in households, communities, and classrooms* (pp. 213–232). Mahwah, NJ: Lawrence Erlbaum Associates.

Bunting, E. (2001) *Gleam and glow.* Illus. Peter Sylvada. New York, NY: Harcourt.

Cahnmann-Taylor, M. & Souto-Manning, M. (2010). *Teachers act up! Creating multicultural learning communities through theatre.* New York, NY: Teachers College Press.

Campano, G. (2012). Keynote Presentation Given at the Toronto Summer Institute. July 3, Mississauga, ON.

Campbell, N.I. & LaFave, K. (2005). *Shi-shi-etko.* Toronto, ON: Groundwood Press.

Chiseri-Strater, E. (1996). Turning in upon ourselves. In P. Mortensen & G. Kirsch (Eds.), *Ethics and representation in qualitative studies of literacy* (pp. 115–133). National Council Teachers of English.

Cochran-Smith, M. & Lytle, S. (1999). The teacher researcher movement: A decade later. *Educational Researcher, 28*(7), 15–25.

Coerr, E. (1986). *Sadako and the thousand paper cranes.* New York, NY: Yearling.

Comber, B. (2001). Negotiating critical literacies. *School Talk, 6*(3), 1–3.

Comber, B. & Nixon, H. (2008). Spatial literacies, design texts, and emergent pedagogies in purposeful literacy curriculum. *Pedagogies: An international journal,* 221–240.

Comber, B. & Simpson, A. (2001). *Negotiating critical literacies in classrooms.* New York, NY: Routledge.

Cooper, K. & White, R.E. (Eds.) (2008). *Critical literacies in action: Social perspectives on teaching practices.* New York, NY: Sense.

Cutler, J. (1999) *The Cello of Mr. O.* Illus. Greg Couch. New York, NY: Dutton.

Darrow, W., Jr. (1970). *I'm glad I'm a boy! I'm glad I'm a girl!* New York, NY: Simon & Schuster.

Demarest, C. (2005). *Alpha, bravo, charlie: The military alphabet.* McElderry.

Dozier, C., Johnston, P., & Rogers, R. (2006). *Critical literacy critical teaching.* New York, NY: Teachers College Press.

Duncan-Andrade, J. & Morrell, E. (2000). *Using hip-hop culture as a bridge to canonical poetry texts in an urban secondary English class.* Paper presented at the Annual Meeting of the American Educational Research Association, New Orleans, LA.

Eco, U. (1970). *The role of the reader.* Bloomington, IN: Indiana University Press.

Edelsky, C. (Ed.) (1999). *Making justice our project: Teachers working toward critical whole language practice*. Urbana, IL: National Council of Teachers of English.

Ewald, W. (2001). *The best part of me: Children talk about their bodies in pictures and words*. New York, NY: Little Brown.

Fairclough, N. (1989). *Language and power*. London: Longman.

Finn, P.J. (1999). *Literacy with an attitude: Educating working-class children in their own self-interest*. Albany, NY: State University of New York Press.

Fleischman, Paul (1997) *Seedfolks*. Illus. Judy Pedersen. New York, NY: HarperCollins.

Flores, B., Cousin, P.T., & Diaz, E. (1991). Transforming deficit myths about learning, language, and culture. *Language Arts*, *68*(2), 369–379.

Frank, B. (2008). Critical literacy. Presentation at InterLERN. Mississauga, ON, Canada. July 18.

Frank, B. (2010). Paper given at the Literacies and Differences Workshop. Mississauga, ON, Canada. July 7.

Freebody, P. & Luke, A. (1990). "Literacies" programs: Debates and demands in cultural context. *Prospect: The Australian Journal of TESOL*, *5*(3), 7–16.

Freire, P. (1970). *Pedagogy of the oppressed*. New York, NY: Herder & Herder.

Freire, P. (2000). *Pedagogy of the oppressed* (30th anniversary edition). New York, NY: Continuum.

Freire, P. & Macedo, D. (1987). *Literacy: Reading the word and the world*. New York, NY: Bergin & Garvey.

Fox, M. (1989). *Feathers and fools*. Illus. Nicholas Wilton. New York, NY: Harcourt Brace.

Gee, J.P. (1999). *An introduction to discourse analysis: Theory and method*. London, UK: Routledge.

Gee, J.P. (1996). *Social linguistics and literacy: Ideology in discourse* (2nd ed.). New York, NY: Taylor & Francis.

Gee, J.P. (2007). *What video games have to tech us about learning and literacy* (2nd ed.). New York, NY: Palgrave Macmillan.

Giroux, H.A. (1996). *Fugitive cultures: race, violence, and youth*. New York, NY: Routledge.

Giroux, H.A. (1994). *Disturbing pleasures: Learning popular culture*. London, UK: Routledge.

Giroux, H. & Giroux, S. (2004). *Take back higher education: Race, youth, and the crisis of democracy in the post-Civil Rights Era*. New York, NY: Macmillan.

Gittens, T., Woo, J., McSweeny, D., & Stovall, L. (Eds.) (2002). *Party animals*. Washington, DC; Wilmington, OH: Orange Frazer Pr Inc.

Hall, S. (1999). Cultural studies and its theoretical legacies. In S. During (Ed.), *The cultural studies reader* (pp. 97–112). New York, NY: Routledge.

Hansen, D. (2007). Ideas, action and ethical vision in education. In D. Hansen (Ed.), *Ethical visions of education: Philosophies in practice* (pp. 1–18). New York, NY: Teachers College Press.

Harste, J.C. (2008a). Do methods make a difference? In M. Lewison, C. Leland, & J.C. Harste, *Creating critical classrooms: K-8 reading and writing with an edge*. Mahwah, NJ: Lawrence Erlbaum Associates.

Harste, J.C. (2008b). Uncertainty and the teaching of reading and writing. In M. Lewison, C. Leland, & J.C. Harste, *Creating critical classrooms: K-8 reading and writing with an edge*. Mahwah, NJ: Lawrence Erlbaum Associates.

Harwayne, S. (1999). *Going public: Priorities and practice at the Manhattan New School*. Portsmouth, NH: Heinemann.

Hess, F. & Leal, D. (2001). A shrinking "digital divide"? The provision of classroom computers across urban school systems. *Social Science Quarterly*, *82*(4), 765–778.

Hinchey, P.H. (1998). *Finding freedom in the classroom: A practical introduction to critical theory.* New York, NY: Peter Lang.

Holmes, R. (2000). *Eyewitness: Battle.* New York, NY: DK Publishing.

hooks, b. (1994). *Teaching to transgress: Education as the practice of freedom.* New York, NY: Teachers College Press.

Janks, H. (2000). Dominance, access, diversity, and design: A synthesis for critical literacy education. *Educational Review, 52*(1), 15–30.

Janks, H. (1993) *Language, identity and power.* Critical Language Awareness Series. Johannesburg: Hodder & Stoughton and Wits University Press.

Janks, H. (2010). *Literacy and power.* New York, NY: Routledge.

Kamler, B. (2001). *Relocating the personal: A critical writing pedagogy.* Albany, NY: State University Press of New York.

Keith, T. (2004) Courtesy of the red, white, & blue (The angry American). *Greatest hits 2.* Dreamworks Nashville. ASIN B00063F8CG.

Kellner, D. & Share, J. (2007). Critical media literacy, democracy, and the reconstruction of education. In D. Macedo & S.R. Steinberg (Eds.), *Media literacy: A reader* (pp. 3–23). New York, NY: Peter Lang.

Kist, W. (2005). *New literacies in action: Teaching and learning in multiple media.* New York, NY: Teachers College Press.

Knobel, M. & Lankshear, C. (Eds.) (2007). *A new literacies sampler.* New York, NY: Peter Lang.

Kress, G. (2003). *Literacy in the new media age.* London, UK: Routledge.

Lakoff, G. (2004). *Don't think of an elephant: Know your values and frame the debate.* White River Junction, VT: Chelsea Green.

Lankshear, C. (1997). Language and the new capitalism. *International Journal of Inclusive Education, 1*(4), 309–321.

Lankshear, C. & Knobel, M. (2003). *New literacies: Changing knowledge and classroom learning.* Buckingham, UK: Open University Press.

Lankshear, C. & McLaren, P.L. (1993). Preface. In C. Lankshear & P.L. McLaren (Eds.), *Critical literacy: Politics, praxis, and the postmodern* (pp. xii–xx). Albany, NY: State University of New York Press.

Larson, J. & Marsh, J. (2005). *Making literacy real: Theories and practices for learning and teaching.* New York, NY: Sage Publications.

Lawton, C. (2004) *Hiroshima: The story of the first atomic bomb.* Sommerville, MA: Candlewick.

Leland, C. & Harste, J. (2000). Critical literacy: Enlarging the space of the possible. *Primary Voices, 9*(1), 3–7.

Leland, C., Lewison, M., & Harste, J.C. (2012). *Teaching children's literature: It's critical!* Mahwah, NJ: Lawrence Erlbaum Associates.

Lester, J. (1998). *From slave ship to freedom road.* Illus. Rod Brown. New York, NY: Dial.

Lewin, K. (1952). *Field theory in social science: Selected theoretical papers by Kurt Lewin.* London, UK: Tavistock.

Lewison, M., Leland, C., & Harste, J.C. (2008). *Creating critical classrooms.* Mahwah, NJ: Lawrence Erlbaum Associates.

Loewen, J. (1996). *Lies my teacher told me.* New York, NY: Touchstone.

Loewen, J. (1999). *Lies across America: What our historic sites get wrong.* New York, NY: The New Press.

Lorbiecki, M. (1998) *Sister Anne's hands.* New York, NY: Dial.

Lortie, D. (1975). *Schoolteacher: A sociological study.* Chicago: University of Chicago Press.

Luke, A. (2007) *Critical literacy.* Toronto, ON: Literacy and Numeracy Secretariat. Available at: http://resources.curriculum.org/secretariat/november29.shtml (accessed January 13, 2013).

Luke, A. (2009). *The new literacies* (Webcast for Educators). Toronto, ON: Curriculum Services Canada.

Luke, A. & Freebody, P. (1997). Shaping the social practices of reading. In S. Muspratt, A. Luke, & P. Freebody (Eds.), *Constructing critical literacies* (pp. 185–223). Cresskill, NJ: Hampton Press.

Luke, C. (2000). New literacies in teacher education. *Journal of Adolescent and Adult Literacy*, *43*(5), 424–435.

Macedo, D. & Steinberg, S.R. (Eds.) (2007). *Media literacy: A reader.* New York, NY: Peter Lang.

MacGinitie, W. (1983). The power of uncertainty. *Journal of Reading*, *5*(1), 677–679.

Marsh, J. (Ed.) (2005). *Popular culture, new media and digital literacy in early childhood.* London, UK: Routledge.

Marshall, E. & Sensoy, O. (Eds.) (2011). *Rethinking popular culture and media.* Milwaukee, WI: Rethinking Schools.

Maruki, T. (1980) *Hiroshima no pika* (The flash of Hiroshima). East Granby, CT: Lothrop.

McIntosh, P. (1989). *White privilege: Unpacking the invisible knapsack.* Wellesley College: Center for Research on Woman.

Mickenberg, J.L. (2010). *Tales for little rebels: A collection of radical children's literature.* New York, NY: NYUPress.

Moll, L.C. (1992). Literacy research in community and classrooms: A sociocultural approach. In R. Beach, J. Green, M. Kamil, & T. Shannahan (Eds.), *Multidisciplinary perspectives in literacy research* (pp. 211–244). Urbana, IL: National Conference on Research in English.

Moody, K. (2007). John culkin, sj: The man who invented media literacy: 1928–1993. Center for Media Literacy. Retrieved from: http://www.medialit.org/reading_room/article408.html.

Morgan, W. (1997). *Critical literacy in the classroom: The art of the possible.* London, UK: Routledge.

Nagle, J. (1999). Social class and school literacy. *Critical literacy in action: Writing words changing worlds* (pp. 159–165). Portsmouth, NH: Boynton/Cook.

National Association for Media Literacy Education (NAMLE) (2007). *Core principles of media literacy education in the United States,* Retrieved from: http://www.amlainfo.org/core-principles.

National Council of Teachers of English (NCTE) (2003). *Resolution on composing with nonpring media.* NCTE Guideline. Retrieved from: http://www.ncte.org/positions/statements/composewithnonprint.

National Council of Teachers of English (NCTE) (2005). *Position statement on multimodal literacies.* NCTE Guideline. Retrieved from: http://www.ncte.org/positions/statements/multimodalliteracies.

National Council of Teachers of English (NCTE) (2008). *Code of best practices in fair use for media literacy education.* NCTE Guideline. Retrieved from: http://www.ncte.org/positions/statements/fairusemedialiteracy.

New London Group (1996). A pedagogy of multiliteracies: Designing social futures. *Harvard Educational Review, 66*(1), 60–92.

Noguera, P. (2008). *The trouble with black boys…and other reflections on race, equity, and the future of public education.* San Francisco, CA: Jossey-Bass.

Pahl, K. & Rowsell, J. (2010). *Artifactual literacies: Every object tells a story.* New York, NY: Teachers College Press.

Peirce, C.S. (1931–58). *Collected writings* (C. Hartshorne, P. Weiss & A.W. Burks, Eds. 8 Volumes). Cambridge, MA: Harvard University Press.

Peterson, R. (2003). Teaching how to read the world and change it: Critical pedagogy in the intermediate grades. In Darder et al. (Eds.), *The critical pedagogy reader* (pp. 365–387). New York, NY: Routledge Falmer.

Pirie, Bruce (1997). *Reshaping high school English.* National Council of Teachers of English.

Rappaport, D. (2004). *Free at last! Stories and songs of emancipation.* Illus. Shane W. Ivans. Sommerville, MA: Candlewick.

Rohmer, H. (1997). *Just like me stories and self portraits by fourteen artists.* New York, NY: Children's Book Press.

Sarder, Z. & Van Loon, B. (1998). *Introducing cultural studies.* New York, NY: Totem.

Sendak, Maurice (1963). *Where the wild things are.* New York, NY: HarperCollins.

Seuss, Dr. (1984). *The butter battle book.* New York, NY: Random House.

Shange, N. (1997). *White wash.* New York, NY: Walker & Company.

Shannon, P. (1995). *Text, lies, & videotape: Stories about life, literacy, & learning.* Portsmouth, NH: Heinemann.

Stein, J., Bock, J., & Harnick, S. (2004). *Fiddler on the roof: Based on Sholom Aleichem's stories.* New York, NY: Limelight.

Sullivan, P. (1996). Ethnography and the problem of the "other". In P. Mortensen & G. Kirsch (Eds.), *Ethics and representation in qualitative studies of literacy* (pp. 97–114). National Council Teachers of English.

Sumara, D. & Davis, B. (1999). Interrupting heteronormativity: Toward a queer curriculum theory. *Curriculum Inquiry, 29*(2), 191–208.

Tan, S. (2007). *The arrival.* New York, NY: Arthur A. Levine Books.

Thomson, P. (2002). *Schooling the rustbelt kids: Making the difference in changing times.* Crows Nest, NSW: Allen & Unwin.

Torres, M. & Mercado, M. (2006). The need for critical media literacy in teacher education. *Educational Studies: A Journal of the American Educational Studies Association, 39*(3), 260–282.

Tucker, N. (2002). Judge orders PETA Party Animal's release: Arts Panel must display group's sad, shackled circus elephant, ruling says. *Washington Post.* August 9.

Vasquez, V. (2004). *Negotiating critical literacy with young children.* New York, NY: Routledge.

Vasquez, V. (2005). *Negotiating critical literacy.* Mahwah, NJ: Lawrence Erlbaum.

Vasquez, V. (2010). *Getting beyond I like the book: Creating spaces for critical literacy in K-9 settings.* Newark, DE: International Reading Association.

Vasquez, V. & Felderman, C. (2013). *Technology and critical literacy in early childhood.* New York, NY: Routledge.

Vasquez, V., Muise, M., Adamson, S., Heffernan, L., Chiola-Nakai, D., & Shear, J. (2003). *Getting beyond I like the book: Creating spaces for critical literacy in K-6 settings.* Newark, DE: International Reading Association.

Walter, V. (1998). *Making up megaboy.* New York, NY: DK Publishing.

Wells, G. (1999). *Dialogic inquiry.* London, UK: Cambridge University Press.

Westheimer, J. & Kahne, J. (2004). What kind of citizen? The politics of educating for democracy. *American Educational Research Journal, 41*(5), 237–269.

Wild, M. (2006). *Fox.* Illus. Ron Brooks. San Diego, CA: Kane Miller.

Wright, C. (2004). On the bumper of my SUV (CD Single). *The Metropolitan Hotel* (Album). Nashville, TN: Dualtone/Painted Red Label.

INDEX